Sunshine and Shenanigans:
Backroad Ramblings with Gramma V

Thank you to all of you who have contributed in EVERY way for this book! I appreciate each of you! May God bless you all (readers included!) in EVERY way! May you see Him in ALL things. And I'm especially grateful to our LOVING GOD who designed us in LOVE and FOR LOVE; He makes all things possible, and all things BEAUTIFUL! . . . Also, the art in the book is mine. I love to get in the "zone" and paint! How about you? . . Well, let the journey begin!

Love, Gramma V

Empty Nest

My summer journeys. What the dickens am I doing traveling the country? Well, the short answer is "because I wanted to!" And the long answer is a bit more emotional and convoluted.

So you know the feeling when school is out and you just want a little vacation? And do some of you parents know the feeling, after you've been a parent for 30-some years, more or less, and all the kids have now left the house and you're wondering what's next? Every day you've been a mom or dad, working out the issues of life and helping your children to launch and then suddenly that vocation is gone?

Maybe you were ecstatic the first time you got a break and the house was quiet, but now the house is usually always quiet and you're not so ecstatic anymore? And you may feel like doing a face plant on your bed and bawling because school is out for the year... actually forever, and you know the next season will be great, but you miss the past years? — you somehow miss the chaos, the challenges, the running, the mess—and . . . all of it?

Well, that was me.

School was out, over, done, finatto—and I needed a "summer vacation" to process my feelings and think about the future.

Yes, I've had an amazing life and so many blessings, and so many wonderful people in it and I love love being a gramma! But this empty nest business kind of hit me sideways.

When we started thinking seriously about selling our house, it seemed a good time to more than visualize a Big Road Trip to see all my people...and all the places I had thought about, and imagined... And why not? ... It's taken months to do it, and variations of plans along the way, but it's been good. God is faithful.

We were in the Tri-cities for a while and my husband has traveled around also. He went to Michigan before I did, to help his mom. We've been blessed that we've been able to be so flexible and so, well, homeless. I recommend it. Do it if you can. Do the things that you want to do when you can. God will work out the details.

We don't know all the reasons why God put us in this time and place, but he has given us our dreams, our desires, our interests, our goals, our talents, etc. One of my friends recently shared that her father-in-law said he thinks God put him on this earth to have fun. In so doing, he helped others to have fun. And that's not a bad thing!

. . . So summer vacation is over. We'll see what's next. I know God is in all the details, as we have seen time and again. Yes, I'll forever miss being a mom. Sometimes I felt like a complete failure, sometimes I felt like I could walk on water, or kiss the moon. Yes, I know I'm still a mom, but it's different.

So, if anyone's listening, hold them close as you give them wings. Enjoy all the moments. Smile at the chaos. Let them know you're listening. . . As I've heard it said—the days are long, but the years are short . . . And then they're over. The door closes one last time as they stride toward their future.

And you wish them well and so much love as the tears run off your chin. And if you're like me, you get in your car and drive away too, looking forward to the next adventure—the open road, the blue skies, the rustling leaves, the rippling lakes, the tall mountains—and all the wonderful people in between.

Enjoying Lancaster County, PA

So here I am in Mennonite/Amish, Pennsylvania... Rolling hills and lovely working farms.... it looks like old McDonald's farm with all the animals, doing what animals do, including pooping on the road as the horses and buggies go flying by.

So many buggies! — did you know there's a little ditch in the pavement where the horses trot along? I didn't realize it until it rained and I was wondering how that ditch got there, and then I saw a horse and buggy go clopping along right in the groove! . . . And so many bicycle riders-I must be careful!

OK, so I don't know how God works things out, or why he does what he does, but . . . I am in Narvon, Pennsylvania at a Mennonite bed-and-breakfast, and someone I "know" comments on my FB photo. He and his wife are good friends with my host family! —and tonight I was invited to dinner with them all—plus another guy whose family I know. All I can say is, small world, BIG God.

So turns out this young man was good friends with my son years ago in North Carolina and visited our home often. I have known his friend's family my whole life... and that's who I had a scrumptious dinner with, (and interesting conversations) around the kitchen table, in a house dating back to 1791. . . God's ways are higher than our ways.

But earlier this morning, I visited with the other guests in the B&B, and was finding a lot of connections with them as fellow believers also. The mom was from Brazil, smiled a lot and didn't speak English, but the daughter was very helpful and suggested various things to do in the area. We finished visiting, and I took my coffee outside to enjoy the morning.

But when I heard the clock-clocking of the buggies rolling by, I quickly ran inside and finished dressing, jumped in my car and started heading to church. Well, when I arrived at what I thought was my host's church, I was feeling reluctant due to all the buggies and dresses and "differentness."

Soon, my hostess texted me and said I could follow her to their church, which was about 15 minutes away. She gave me the address and I met her there. She's such a kind sweet little mama. There are lots of churches here, glad I found the right one.

Surprising, I felt comfortable in church. The message I heard was to live by the golden rule—treating others how I wanted to be treated. Another message I heard was not to judge others, unless we want to be judged by the same measuring stick. I also heard not to worry about the small speck in someone else's eye – that we don't know what they're going through, the burden they are bearing.

I'm glad my hostess whispered to me when they were about to pray because all the sudden everybody hit the floor on their knees, so I joined them, of course. They must do exercises as they age to keep agile!

The church was so light and airy, lots of ceiling fans and windows. I didn't recognize the songs from their song book. Afterwards, I asked the ladies who the guys were sitting at the table in the middle, and they smiled and said those were the song leaders. Then it all made sense. They were just like the Finnish "loukedes" from my early memories. They further explained that the church song books don't have notes. The song leaders will choose a (familiar) melody to sing with the hymn, isn't that interesting? And all the congregation paused between each verse, then the song leaders led off, and then everyone else joined in.

After church I visited with some ladies. Pretty print dresses for the ladies, and interesting outfits for the men. The guys go out one door, and the ladies go out the other door to visit, and never the twain shall meet.

It's a very sweet community and God is good and for some reason, he wants us to connect and do life together. So here I am thinking . . . life is short. God wants us to bless others, and others to bless us. It's good to engage.

Later I was sitting under a tree as the raindrops pattered on my windshield, working on my pictures, and I heard a familiar clop, clop, so I popped out of my car and got a video of another buggy. They're so fascinating, and the lifestyle is interesting. I'm not sure why I'm so enamored by it, maybe it has to do with my growing up years on the farm, and my early fascination with many historical figures—Laura Ingalls, etc., and history in general—the settlers, building of America, all the hopes and dreams for a better life.

Another thing I'm finding on my cross-country journey is, we have more in common than we have differences. I learned this in school, and it's true in life. Sitting down and talking with people or standing outside, (me in pants, with painted nails, them in modest print dresses, wearing little white caps) chatting with the Mennonite gals after church—it was easy to find commonalities. It was easy to look into their eyes and smile as we talked about children, where we came from and life. They smiled back, and, I felt connected.

I also felt a sense of belonging as I walked to my black car in a sea of all the other black cars.
Not all Mennonite orders have black cars, some ride in buggies and bicycles, others have a variety of colored cars. They're just like the rest of us, we migrate to where we feel comfortable.

The last thing I want to comment on today is the interesting rocks with which many of the older homes are built—a combination of Ironstone and other building materials, they turn orange because they rust. The B&B I'm staying in is painted white over the rocks—hence the name of the B&B-Iron Stone Farm. So what I believed happened was—as early settlers were clearing fields, they gathered the rocks and built their homes. The house I'm staying in was built in 1791. The host's grandmother lived here as a little girl.

It's such an interesting house and a beautiful well-kept farm with lots going on. Cats, dogs, milking cows in the milking barn and a pond hiding somewhere—I will leave that discovery for another time.

Well, God bless you all, my sweet friends in Pennsylvania and beyond. Until we meet again.

Traveling through Frankenmuth

It's fun to travel and be out and about, seeing new things, experiencing different aspects of our world, to see how other people live.

Blue skies and puffy, white clouds... My favorite kind of day :-)... I've always loved a road trip and I've been tripping most of the summer :-)... Living the dream, well, my dream—talking with nice folks, stopping at farm stands and traveling in the slower lane. Seeing what there is to see. Of course, life is full of ups and downs. It's all part of this life and God helps us along.

I went to a town called Frankenmuth— a Bavarian Village. The original settlers were from Germany, and they brought their colorful flare with them. Downtown and around, everything was so beautiful, full of flowers and good cheer.

I took a steamboat ride down the Cass River, which empties into Lake Huron and has tributaries all up the Upper Peninsula. There's lots to see and take in. I learned some things about snapping turtles and about steamboats in general. I drank a soda and ate some popcorn—dropping pieces in the river like Hansel and Gretel.

I drove over a wooden covered bridge. Then, I enjoyed my gorgeous charcuterie board at a little bistro. I bought some jams and jellies and a few other doodads. I went into Bronner's -the largest Christmas store ever, and was just totally overwhelmed!

Of course, I found the clearance section.

And then like a homing pigeon, I hopped in my car, said a prayer and hit the road.

Some Really Good News!

Hey, do you want to hear some good news? Actually, I mean Blow-Your-Mind good news?!

God loves us, He loves us, He loves us!!

He sings over us with JOY!

His banner over us is LOVE.

He smiles at us . . . Yes, that's right.

He delights in us!

He has ordained good paths for us to walk in; He has GOOD plans for our lives.

He is always with us.

He has given us the MIND of CHRIST!

The Creator of the Universe wants to spend ETERNITY with us. - The intimate Creator-God just wants to sit down with us and chat. . . amazing!

He stretched out His arms and died so that we might LIVE forever! His blood washes us clean.

He has sealed us with His seal (it is on our foreheads-HOLY to the LORD).

Our names are engraved in His palms and written in His book of LIFE!

His thoughts toward us are like the sands of the sea . . .

Wow.

And that's the short list!!

So, are we going to let a tempering wanna-be god called satan define us and our lives? Render us useless and ineffective by his continual lies and taunts and temptations to sin!? To doubts and fears and what- ifs? To always be looking at the ugly he is causing in this world?

Are you KIDDING? Get behind us satan! You are a wanna-be, a liar, deceiver, an enemy from the beginning! Christ has already crushed your head. Crushed! The victory is ours through Jesus. We are MORE than conquerors in Christ. ALL of our needs are provided in HIM. Every single one. And you know what? He says, "Test me, try me. Taste and see that I AM GOOD."

Hallelujah! Praises to the KING of KINGS!!

. . . Walk in that FREEDOM, and JOY and LIGHT and LIFE, my friends. The freedom that is ours in CHRIST JESUS.

He has set us free. We are free indeed!

Rejoice! Sing praise! Glory to His name!

Heading "Home" to the Upper Peninsula

I had been out and about and then I had the pleasure of driving toward my temporary home. All day it felt better and better. The air seemed to get clearer, the traffic thinned out. Beautiful color began to appear in the trees.

I was heading toward small-town America and I was loving it!

I whizzed my windows down and zoomed along. The day had turned sunny blue by the time I was crossing the 5-mile-long Mackinac bridge. I didn't even cringe as I looked down at all that water under me. (I just said a prayer and hung onto the wheel!)

I found my lovely place to stay for the night, Lake Huron waves were rolling up on the shore, and I listened to them all night long. So wonderful!

I felt happy to be going "home." In a way it feels really strange not to know how long we will be in the Upper Peninsula of Michigan, or what's next, but the sense of "home" is strong.

Alaska Bound!

Today I sat with some of sister Liz's people. Liz is such a kind, generous person, she helps many people wherever she goes. She listens and learns from others how they live and navigate their lives, in the last frontier of Alaska. I listened to their stories too. I looked in their faces and saw their grit, their passion, their determination.

We looked back over the years together. In one case, back to Michigan, not far from where my parents grew up.

The year was around 1950. The family owned 600 acres of

farmland, 200 was planted with potatoes. Harvest time came and the large family worked hundreds of hours; they stacked the potatoes up in a row a mile long, 30 feet high... Millions of potatoes. Their best year ever.

They had them sold for $.75 a bushel to a large contractor. Government officials showed up and told them they would be paid $.25 a bushel. The farmer looked at his wife and children - still dusty from the work of harvesting those potatoes.

The Farmer tried to reason with the government officials, "We've already got them sold for $.75 a bushel." The government official shook his head "no" and told them that the officials were going to mark the potatoes with purple dye and if any showed up at market, the farmer would be greatly fined.

The potatoes would be left to rot. . . 200 acres worth.

The farmers went to bed and the young boy heard his mother and father crying in their bedroom down below. In the morning, the parents told the children the news, "We're selling out and moving west."

They had an auction and everything was sold. The family bought two big dump trucks and headed west. They got to the point in Montana where the road headed north to Alaska, but they were on their way to Washington or Oregon. A stranger at the gas stop asked the farmer where they were going with those dump trucks and told him they were needed in Alaska. The family discussed their options and turned their wheels north.

They traveled mostly over dirt roads; many rivers had no bridges. They finally arrived in Alaska and worked - hauling with their trucks. They started growing roots. They came back to the states once more for a winter before buying a homestead on the Kenai Peninsula. The family grew and dispersed over the area, some moved back to the lower 48. They became landowners, longshoremen, fishing merchants, businessmen-and women. Families. Families that make up the backbone of the land of the free and the home of the brave.

And that's one story of how Alaska was populated by the brave hearty folks who call it home. Hearty folks with lots of grit.

No Small Potatoes

This is a small potato story, with a big heart.

I love my grandkids to the moon! —with good reason. They are all so sweet, smart, generous, silly and just so fun to be with!

The ones who lived close to me in Washington, would always come bursting in the door, with smiles (and maybe a little jam) on their faces. More times than not, they would have a note, a book or some other treasure to share.

On this particular day, one of the little gals handed me her purple and white striped little purse. I looked inside. There were about 6 average looking potatoes. I looked again. There was also one tiny one—about the size of a walnut.

I smiled at little Miss. She said, "They're for you, Gramma, I got them from my garden." That year, the littles had their own gardens to take care of.

I just about burst there on the spot! . . . Here's this tiny little gal, with her treasures tucked into her white and purple purse, for Gramma! . . . And that one little one . . . "No potato left behind," I thought. . . That is just too precious. I could imagine her little hands digging through the damp earth gathering her treasures, including that wee little potato, right along with the big ones!

Nope. There's no "small potatoes." Everything and everyone has significance.

Whether you are a person or a potato, everyone and everything matters.

Beautiful Michigan Summer

These beautiful summer days
of rolling Michigan hills and swaying grass,
of peaceful grazing cattle
of rustling leaves in homey white birch.
Mellow old sheltering barns nestle
cozily into small valleys,
warming in the sun
bales of hay sit ready for the coming storms.
But still the breezes whisper
the sun smiles on glowing skin and flitting birds fishing at the pond.
The lakes ripple, inviting one more swim
cold layers below the dappled waves.
Crunchy apples ripen on weathered limbs
gold flows into amber in the evening sky
as these golden summer days
contentedly fade into love and happy memories.

Feeling my Roots in Eagle River

Oh, this little gem! . . .This small harbor town called Eagle River, it is in a place like this, where I could let my roots sink deep . . . slowly coasting down the road less traveled, on a path marked "dead end." (But it's so rich and alive!!)

Past the flower boxes on porches filled with yellow petunias, past the rustling wind-bent trees, past the sweet cabins and mellow cottages, down to the lakeshore, and the rolling endless surf.

I wonder, why they ever left—my mother from Chassell and my father from Ironwood—surrounded by the Great Lake Superior. This jewel, this gem of sparkling water and rocks painted red in the surf. White sand beaches and long coves dotted with cottages and hardy folks, young and old, walking in the sand and smiling into the sun.

These lucky people, these natives—The gentleman from Chicago sweeping his porch and the sweet lady from California, enjoying their summer homes here in this beautiful place. There's the serene Gitche Gumme (Ojibwa for big water) Camp, the apple orchard, the whispering Falls and the "the dragonfly cottage." All the places to invite adventure and imagination.

Some folks stopping to buy jam from "the jam lady" or to eat at the Fitzgerald restaurant—named after the great ship sunk at sea— in this first port established at the beginning of the copper mining boom in 1845.

But now... this restored tiny cove, with massive historic buildings on the sturdy bluff above, watching over the sea that rolls fierce and wild in the winter, but gently undulates in the waning summer sun.

Ending are Hard, God is Faithful

It's been a good day—filled with good things and wonderful people, blue puffy skies and the best Ambassador pizza, church with family and friends, fun and crafts with the grands, beautiful vistas, time at Anita's bedside with family, a nap, a swim in Chassell Bay . . . all the good good things, and yet . . . Yet, I have a lump in my throat, tears loom.

Grief is real and we all suffer in this life. Yes, there's joy and gladness, shouts of laughter and jokes and many sweet times. For those I give thanks! But somehow, we are called to give thanks in ALL things.

And those "all things" is where I struggle.

The suffering. The sadness. The life draining from a vibrant body. Hearing the difficulties of so many— past and present. The dashed dreams. The broken relationships. The sorrow. The life cut too short, or sometimes seemingly too long—aching for those long gone.

We get just one life. . . and sometimes it seems we reap what we sow. But other times, the pattern seems so random. Why? The "good marriages," the difficult ones. The God-loving children, the ones who suffer in so many ways. Healthy active bodies and minds, sickness and struggles. The long lives, the ones seemingly taken too soon. The joy today, the sorrow tomorrow.

This makes me think of Ecclesiastes. There is nothing new under the sun. Vanity, vanity all is vanity. But what does that mean and how does it help us navigate life?

I guess I'm thinking, contemplating—and that's ok. I know God is good; His name is faithful and true...We can trust our God.

And that's where I land. . . Trusting God with all of it. He's the One who gave me life, who breathed his breath into my nostrils. He's the One who sustains me and helps me and loves me best. He's the One who set the universe on its course, and will see us through to the end of this age, and beyond.

So I invite Him into my feelings, into this angst. This knowing that I will have tribulations beyond my control in this life. That life will hurt. That children will suffer. That moms will struggle. That friends will grieve. That death will come.

So, as He leads, I will continue to trust His word, His truth, His ways, His heart.

. . . And I will leave the rest with Him as we wait for the Coming Age that has no end—when our True life begins!

New Mercies Every Morning

I love, love, love a new morning, don't you? The day is fresh and full of hope and potential. It's like the Bible says, his mercies are new every morning. How awesome is that? A whole clean day, just waiting to be enjoyed. In which to be blessed and to be a blessing to others. (Lam. 3:22-23)

My children and I used to listen to positive encouraging messages on the way to and from school. It was only about five minutes each way, but wow, what a difference it makes! The kids can relate to the stories being told and it's all about "I think I can, I think I can," rather than "I can't do this, I'm worthless, in fact I can't do anything." The power of life and death is in the tongue. It's in the words we speak and the messages we believe about ourselves and our world. They make the difference. (Prov. 18:21)

And it's not that we need to "win" every time, in every situation, or even look successful in the world's eyes. We experience satisfaction when we are doing our personal best, giving it our all, and resting in Jesus. It's then, that we experience "success." What a difference to start the day with positive thoughts. "I can do all things through Christ. I have the mind of Christ. He will work all things for my good. He is kind and merciful. He sings over me with JOY! His good thoughts for me are more numerous than the sands of the sea. He has created good paths for me to walk in!!!" Oh my. Oh my! Thank you, LORD. (Phil. 4:13, 1 Cor. 2:16, Rom. 8:28, Ps. 145:17, Ps. 139:17-18, Eph. 2:10)

I will pour out my tribute of praise to you, joyful merciful Abba. Blessings to all! Be blessed as you experience God's FULLNESS.

It's Summer when the Curlings Come

It's summertime . . . The cousins who live away are here! Well, some of them. . . We are all missing our Jonny boy (oh Jonny boy). It's always a good time when the Curlings are around.

We do all the fun things! There's lots of laughter and swimming and fun and walks and sitting around the fire. And we remember those who have run on ahead, seemingly too early, but our days on this earth are numbered by our Creator even before they begin. So those of us who remain, grieve with Hope and we hug a little tighter and laugh a little longer.

We forgive quicker and we remember to give thanks to our God who gently leads us along. We all have our special memories— one of mine is the kids sitting around playing games...playing games and laughing. Quelf was a specialty. And beach and sand and sun—that was Jon—forever young. We carry his memory with us. We love you Jonny and all of the rest of our Curling family.

You make the world a brighter better place and you bring the soft sweet days of Summer when you come.

Logging in the Winter: UP Style

My mother's family's roots run deep in the Upper Peninsula of Michigan.

There's the dilapidated home where mom was born, on the edge of the woods. There's the home where her grandparents settled by Otter Lake in Tapiola, Michigan. There's Gramma's former home on the hill in Chassell. The graves in the Ello Cemetery. And there's Karvakko's Store out in Tapiola.

My great-grandfather, John Carl Dryge (later changed to Carl Olson) was born in Pajala, Sweden. He came to America in the late 1800's and settled in Minnesota, but left when a tornado blew down their buildings. When he and his bride (Christina Niva – possibly Lars Levi Laestadius' granddaughter) saw Otter Lake, she was so infatuated with the similar scenery of her birthplace in Muonio Lapland that she wanted to settle there. They built their home and started farming.

Carl hurt his leg in a logging accident, so he started a grocery business in what became Karvakko's. Business was booming. Then a swindler from a silver fox farm approached him with a convincing plan to make fistfuls of money raising silver foxes for their pelts. Carl invested everything he had. When it came time to sell the pelts, they were almost worthless.

In financial ruin, Carl was forced back into the logging industry in his declining years. By this time, he had remarried Ida Peterson, widow of Jeremia. One winter he had a sizable number of logs to be sledded down to the Worcester railroad, when a monstrous blizzard filled in the road to a depth of several feet, so that it was impossible to open it up.

Carl went to the hardware stores in town and bought a sleigh load of snow shovels and hired an army of workers to handle them. The road was opened, although it was 2 miles long. The logs would have been ruined, but they all made it to the landing to be sold.

I am thankful for my strong heritage of Finnish Sisu.

Brides and the Brevity of Life

I was thinking of brides and the brevity of life.

I'm here in the UP helping to care for my mother-in-law, Anita Walikainen, along with her children Gregg and Betsy. Yesterday as we all got together for lunch with Anita's brother, Stan, I thought it would be fun to be up here in the Upper Peninsula of Michigan, Just having a great summer—doing all the wonderful Michigan things.

However, Anita has terminal pancreatic cancer. She's not in pain, but is tired and weak. So we take care of her needs.

Life is funny. Funny probably isn't the right word because I'm tearing up as I write this.

I've been working on Anita's life story and getting pictures together. As I scroll through the pictures on my phone, her life passes before my eyes in a few moments.

That's the "funny" part of life, it seems to take forever sometimes, but it truly passes in a flash. The Bible says our life is a breath.

Just a breath here on this planet. Then forever in eternity.

She is a beautiful blessing to so many. A truly kind person, who exemplifies the Love verse in the Bible. She is kind and patient. She is not envious, she doesn't brag, nor is she proud. She behaves appropriately, and thinks of the interest of others. She is not easily provoked, nor does she rejoice in unrighteousness. She bears all things, believes all things, hopes all things and endures all things.

Even this. Even cancer.

Please pray with us for her continued comfort and peace and good health to the end. She is at peace and is resting in God's provision.

She's a beautiful person whose life is a blessing to those around her.

As I look at her life pictures, I can see that Life truly is just a breath. Sometimes long, sometimes short, but still, just a breath.

And then eternity.

For her, and those who know Jesus as Lord and Savior, it will be a beautiful new LIFE! Forever as the bride of Christ.

Our Identity in Christ
. . . made in the image of God. Gen 1:26&27

. . . a child of God. John 1:12

. . . a temple – a dwelling place of God. 1 Cor. 3:16

*. . . chosen, holy, blameless, adopted, forgiven, redeemed,
    sealed by God, declared a saint. Eph. 1:3-14*

. . . righteous and holy. Eph. 4:24

*. . . chosen and appointed by Christ to bear his fruit.
     John 15:16*

*. . . God's handiwork born anew in Jesus to do good works.
     Eph 2:10*

. . . chosen of God, holy and dearly loved. Col 3:12

. . . will resemble Christ when he returns. 1John 3:1-2

. . . fearfully and wonderfully made. Ps. 139:14

. . . God's treasured possession. Duet. 14:2

. . . loved and filled with the fullness of God. Eph. 3:17-19

. . . justified by faith. Gal. 2:16

. . . reconciled to God, holy, and blameless. Col. 1:22

*. . . salt, light, created for good works and God's glory
     Matt. 5:13-16*
. . . good plans for future and hope. Jer. 29:11

The Boy in the Yellow Pants

So we were sitting in the patio seating, being pestered by a wasp while I was digging in my wallet for a gift certificate for my youngest son. I came across his high school graduation picture. I showed it to him and said proudly, "That's my boy."

"A mere child," he said, with all the salt of a Lord of the Rings aficionado.

So I guess he now thinks he's all grown up with his nice black dress shoes, his coiffed curly hair and his sleeve of tattoos. This birthday boy of mine.

After we ate, he drove me across the street and showed me the bachelor pad that he shares with a couple of other dudes. One was making chicken in the Insta Pot and the other was gaming. I saw a couple decks of different card games on the round table in the dining area and guess what?

The place was clean!

For the sake of his honor, I won't go into details, but I thought of all those years of harping at him about the condition of his room growing up.

I wanted to both laugh and cry. What in the world?! Does all the worrying and harping matter? -The condition of the room as a reflection of the way a person deals with life? Should a parent just close the door, back out and never say a word? When they're grown and gone you wonder about those kinds of things.

Driving home I was thinking about my son and the man he is becoming. My heart swelled a little and squeezed some tears out of my eyes.

I thought of all the school years, editing papers and helping him finish up high school in the midst of Covid. I thought of all the swords and shields he made . . . How he would want me to fence with him. When I got tired, he would say, "Just sit there mom and hold up your sword," and he would whack away at it.

He was always a sharp dresser. Even when he was little and begged me to make him some bright yellow pants that matched one of his play characters. He insisted on the little sheath that would hold his small purple butter knife from the Little Tykes playset. He was armed and ready for battle! He loved his pants so much that he wore them that night to Leslie Stenersen's calling hours.

That was the same night that his dad was working in the sound booth. One of the church ladies walked in and stopped at the pew where he was working. She looked over at Gregg and said, "Oops! My slip just fell off. What should I do?" And he said, like any everyday-undergarment-counselor would say, "step out of it and put it in your purse."

She did. And life went on.

Life goes on.

While I was riding home, I also thought about that graduation picture and the "photo shoot" that produced it. That was me taking pictures on my cell phone down at the pond across the field from our house. That's how things went for us. That was his graduation photo shoot.

Sometimes it seems like we lived life on a wing and a prayer, flying by the seat of our pants, cobbling things together as we went.

We weren't polished and prepped, doing all the right things, getting our kids in the right sports, the right schools, the best gigs. But we lived life the best we could.

We made pants, we laughed, we cried, we took senior pictures at the pond across the field. We held up our swords, sometimes sitting down to do it.

And it must've been good enough. Because there was a boy who's grown into a man who can make his bed and tie his shoes. He knows how to work for the things he wants in life.

He's kind and considerate. He's a good friend. His tattoos speak of faith and Jesus and his cousin who ran ahead to glory.

And I think I'll stop now because my heart is doing that thing to my eyes again.

Happy birthday son! Keep looking up . . . and thanks for all the great years. Thanks for visualizing the yellow pants.

Love and Life and Legacy

"To mother dear" the faded blue card read.

The shaggy-furred bears looked on from eyes ragged and worn; they seemed to understand.

Books and tattered dolls, blessed by small hands squeezing them tight. Old pictures, beloved photos, baby clothes—treasured and loved, kept as precious memories. Mementos of days gone by. Souvenirs of trips to the lake, skating on the pond and building the snowmen.

There's a lifetime here in this mis-matched pile of fabric, paper and glass. I couldn't just put them in a bag and send them away! Not yet anyway. Somehow, it seems right to gather a few together to represent the years. To remember.

To imagine the tea parties and ball games, the conversations over mashed potatoes and roast beef. To see the smiling eyes, wrinkles growing in the once-smooth faces. To picture the sun-burnt noses and the big blue eyes.

To hear the doors slam and the bike horns squeak. To remember the hopes and dreams of those who lived and breathed and cried and laughed—gone on ahead, and all this they left behind. And, oh so much more!

The mind grapples with the meaning of life. The legacies. The hopes and fears. The tears. The joy. The pain. The love.

These bits and pieces of a human existence have elements of all those emotions – wrapped up in the scraggly fur, the wobbly letters, the worn-out clothing. They speak of love and life and legacy.

The ones who have gone before are not forgotten. Love beat hard in their chests too!

Laughter exploded from their lips. Anger shot through their veins. Wonder tumbled around in their brains. Their minds and hands committed to the tasks at hand. They toiled and struggled—were defeated and overcame.

Just like us. These ancestors of ours who kept the dolls and the bears, the letters and the trucks.

This certainly isn't just a pile of old junk, mangled and soiled. This speaks of a life well-lived, tenderly packed away, as the years slowly passed by.

So, as I clear the attic and the basement, the drawers and cupboards, I honor those who have passed and those who are no longer young. I will remember for them— the love, the years, the passing, and also the meaning of life.

The meaning is love. Love—that's what it's all about. God is love. He created us in love, for love. For today, tomorrow and forever. And because He loves, we can love.

It is love that lives on—through it all. And it's love that made the meals and washed the dishes, sang to the children and tucked them in at night. It's love that gathered the abandoned toys and washed the clothes and placed them in the box. And all the rest is love too—the albums and tea cups and the memories.

Down Syndrome Perfection

Awhile back, I was privileged to teach a class of 20 sweet kindergartners. Even at that age, they all come with a unique personality, gifts, and a way of viewing and interacting with the world. The day progressed smoothly with my helper-of-the-day being my right-hand girl. She kept me in line and told me details such as who gets what markers (that's important information, you know) and on what line we walk to recess.

Shy smiles and willing hands tackled the 1-2-3 counting math project. They colored, cut, and glued. They diligently blew their noses and washed with hand sanitizer when I reminded them to do that instead of snuffling and picking boogers. Oh yes, each reminder sent 5-10 kids to the back of the room to take care of that little detail.
Yes, this small band of children blessed me with their smiles, words, and deeds.

But, none more than a little boy whose 21st chromosome is a little different than most people's.

It was reading time and I found a book titled, "I like me."
Perfect, I thought. Positive messages.

We gathered in a circle and got ready for the reading adventure.

The book started out with the statement, "I like me." Knowing
how important it is to have self-like at the center of our being, I
asked the children to repeat the sentences as we read. They
agreed. Every sentence I read was followed by a chorus of
voices. Super sweet. Especially when the pig in our story said, "I
like my curly tail, my round tummy, and my pointy toes." (Some
of the kids had to wiggle their little bums on the tail part.)

The book went on about making mistakes, trying and trying
again, feeling sad, and making myself feel better. All good
advice. All necessary advice to being able to cope and self-
regulate throughout life.

My little down-syndrome boy had sat at the edge of the circle,
but once we got part-way into reading and talking about how
everyone is special and how we like me and we like each other,
he scooched his little rump closer into the group. He smiled
between his missing teeth, pushing his black-rimmed glasses
back on his nose. Voice clear, he repeated the positive
messages with pleasure.

The final words of the story were, "I like me." As I read them, I
closed the book and smiled at the class. They all repeated it
back. However, the spectacled cherub smiled a big grin and
said, "I like you!"

I smiled back and replied, "I like you too!" Most of the kids then
said similar nice things to me and the other children. And then
we went on to our next task.

Sweet, I thought.

But, later, I thought something more.

I thought, here was a little boy, who is different from his classmates, who seemed to already have learned one of the most vital lessons of life. You see, he already liked himself enough, was so confident in who he was, that he could freely give and share love and affirmation. And he didn't even have to think about it. Or spend years grappling with it.

It kind of blew me away.

At five, he had by-passed a huge hang-up of self-identity and self-worth. He was secure in who he was. And it allowed him to love others with abandon.

Wow.

Different? Special? Talented? Lovely? Perfect?

I would say so.

Like you, Jesus. Help us to see others as you do.

Two Old Friends

The two long-time friends greeted each other—one from her wheelchair, the other leaning on a cane. One said "I wondered who that old lady was, coming up the walk with her cane." The other replied, "I wondered, 'who is that old woman sitting in the wheelchair?'"

Trying to give them some privacy, the others in the house sat a distance away to visit in the sun-splashed kitchen. The friends hugged, smiled, and then settled in for what was probably their last time of fellowship this side of glory. These two have shared much—children being born, raised, and moving on; Bible studies; church functions; and family visits. All that is waning, along with the vitality of life, but their shared faith in the One who is always with them, carries them through their days.

They have each laid a husband to rest and have continued on alone, blessing their families. They have been an inspiration and encouragement to many. The end is nearer for one than the other, but both are still holding on to the joys of this present life—friendship, family, faith, sunshine, flowers, fellowship, and good-will.

As we were leaving, the frail lady from the chair made sure we were given a parting gift. I don't believe anyone leaves her door empty-handed, this woman who raised ten thriving children. However, the gifts this time were not the making of her hands, but of her daughter's.

A picture of this lovely lady, in the bloom of youth, sits on a high shelf. She smiles from the picture, decked in her wedding gown, her groom is standing and he is smiling. They are beautiful. But no more beautiful than she is now, a bride adorned with a perfect robe of righteousness. She is ready to meet her eternal groom, the One who is standing, waiting to receive her. She assured me, "I am at peace. God is with me. If I die in my sleep, I know that I will wake up with Jesus." The wedding bells will ring soon and there will be no crying there.

This devotion was written about my mother Mary and her dear friend Clara who have now both gone on to glory.

Daily Wisdom to Self-Care

Repeat throughout the day:

Finally, brethren, whatsoever things are true, whatsoever things are honest, whatsoever things are just, whatsoever things are pure, whatsoever things are lovely, whatsoever things are of good report; if there be any virtue, and if there be any praise, think on these things. (Phil 4:8)

Release the happy endorphins . . . Exercise every day!

Do something fun . . . Laugh! Create!

Help your body . . . Eat greens!

Get plenty of rest . . . (zzzzz)

Be kind to yourself and others . . . it makes everyone happy!

Think good thoughts . . . you are worthy of love and you belong. You are essential to being alive in your place in the world!

Breathe . . . Deeply, in and out, in and out. . .

Selling the House, God is our Sanctuary

Today I'm remembering and giving thanks. Today I am thankful for house and home, for friends and family, for faith, hope and love.

In life, there are times of laughter and times of sorrow. We are so blessed that God is with us through it all. Time passes, people come and go through the doors of our homes and through our lives. Our house has sold and we will be moving on.

I want to remember the way the sun shown in the windows, walks to the pond and how the trees rose to the skies. I want to remember the birds on the fence, my rosemary bush covered in snow and the children splashing in the pool. I will remember cooking and baking, parties and camp fires. I will remember children getting their first cars, traveling to new places and experiencing life.

There have been happy times when our older relatives, siblings, children and grands have filled my kitchen and our small backyard— shouts of laughter and some shouts of deep grief too. (Even silly faces as someone pinched someone else's bum during a family photo!) I remember children and grands coming and going— some moving out, some moving back, weddings, funerals and birthdays. Today I'm remembering with gratitude all the memories we have shared here in our beautiful home.

Mom passed one year ago today and Jonny has been gone for a year and a half; we broke bread and shared life with them and many others in the home that God provided for this time. Now it's time for a new chapter, a new season. I'm thankful that God is with us through it all. He is our sustaining peace, our lasting place of refuge, our sanctuary.

A Few Gems from the Blueberry Field

Years ago, I had the opportunity to work for a weekend at my uncle's blueberry farm—assigning picking spots, weighing buckets, taking money, and giving out "blueberry advice." Such as good recipes and how to best keep the berries.

On our first day of work, my daughter and I headed over to the blueberry field early in the morning. As we unloaded our supplies in the morning mist and set up the blueberry stand, I glanced over at Charlie, the pet mastiff. He gave a woof and flopped down at the end of his leash—he was ready to do some serious relaxing. He looked quite tame now and is really as meek as a lamb, but Charlie is pretty scary looking when he comes charging at you, barking, with spittle flying everywhere.

Throughout the day, many interesting pickers came and went. Most people came to pick berries with a child or two. Some children jumped into the task whole-heartedly, others did not. They wandered around, took trips to the bathroom, and came up for drinks of water— two or five times. But most of these little people were agreeable and interesting. Maybe it's the grandma in me, but little kids are just so fascinating! Their bouncing curls, chubby cheeks, and little hands are so precious. One little girl came up with a flower on a stem that was as tall as she was—she had found a treasure. Later in the day, I noticed a little boy looking longingly at Charlie and gave him a friendly wave good-bye. What happens to us? How do we lose the wonder of living and enjoying the simple pleasures?

Of course, people come to the berry field to harvest delicious berries, but I think they also come for something more. During the day, I had time to tie on a bucket and do a little picking myself. I found that a person can lose themselves in a berry bush. The wind whispers, the sun dazzles, the bees buzz, and I kind of forgot that I live in the twenty-first century, with twenty-one things weighing me down. An earthy freedom captivated my mind, the hunter/gatherer rises to the challenge, and my cares just seemed to float away on the breeze.

But. . . all good things must end. And so it was with our day in the berry field. Our last customer waved good-bye; we closed down the stand, and headed home. A little weary, a lot dirty, and a little freer to just . . .enjoy the natural blessings that a day in a country berry patch brings. (Ecc. 3:1-8)

Love Never Fails

Love never fails. I woke up in the night with these words in my mind and it seemed like God spoke a sermon to me right there in my flannel sheets!

The scripture was just opened up – it was so real and vibrant. The thought was with me that even if everything else fails, LOVE never will. GOD's love never fails. We humans cannot even begin to comprehend the magnitude of this divine love, but we try.

God's design for love is illustrated in the 13th chapter of 2nd Corinthians. I had read this chapter earlier in the day, because I knew I should spend some time in the Word. I read and read, but it just seemed like words on a page. Dry.

Now that I think about it, that is an example of MY love – out of duty, wooden, just going through the motions, doing it because I "should." But! My faithful God woke me up in the night to lavish HIS love on me – His penitent child.

Isn't He good?! LOVE NEVER FAILS. Place emphasis on any one word and there is so much to contemplate. So, I encourage you, go read 2nd Corinthians, chapter 13 and see how God blesses your day – and your night. His name is Faithful and True!

Remembering on the Water's Edge

During my wanders home, I love stopping at the water to say hello. My sister said the water is in our DNA. Our parents grew up on the banks of Lake Superior. Different towns. Different experiences. Sweet memories that gently call.

We remember, time passes. We wear scarves on our heads now

instead of tiny swimsuits. So here we are, on the banks of childhood memories again. Seems like One always returns, doesn't it?

We return to the places of grief and of comfort. Our parents are now both gone (how can that even be?), the home place just up the road holds others, but the memories live on—and here we are, at the water's edge, taking in the things of "home."

The geese honk and paddle, the water laps, the wind whistles, the sky dazzles. We pick up sticks, "hear" the sizzle of hot dogs over the fire, family all around— and then we walk away—the memories gently playing like an old movie softly clicking, slow motion. We make our way through the tall evergreens leaving the lake behind.

We were so full of the adventures to come; we dashed to the water's edge and swam without fear, we smiled into the sun. And then today we came to feel it again—two "oldish" ladies, wrapped in scarves and drifting memories.

Covenant Love – Hesed

Today I'm thanking God for his covenant love – hesed. The kind of love that says he is steadfast in his lovingkindness. The kind of love that says he will never break his covenant with us.

When we become his, he enters a covenant relationship with us that cannot be changed by our behavior. This covenant relationship is not dependent on our performance; all the responsibility lies with God! If you doubt, check out David's life.

And now God promises that he will treat us according to the faithful mercies shown to David. Hallelujah! Yes, I'm thanking

God for his covenant love that He shares with us. I'm praying for His love and joy to come bouncing out of heaven and land "splat! plop!" on all of us!

May you be splatted and plopped with showers and waves of love and joy today!   (1 Chro. 17) (Ps. 51) (Ps. 23)

Ode to an Automobile

She slowly lumbered down the lane, old Curby, who had served us well. Her powerful engine purred, then roared as she faithfully responded to pressure on her gas pedal. That was old Curby—faithful to last. Gas-guzzling, far-too-wide for most parking places, and old-as-the-hills, I knew I'd miss her as I watched her taillights disappear down the driveway for the last time. (As a farm girl, she reminded me of an old cow, being put out to pasture.) Even though she was painted green (minus a fee dings and scratches) the footprint she left was way too big for this new generation that values "green" as a concept, rather than a color. Curby had served our six kids and us well, but her time of service was over.

Why did she pull at my heart as she rumbled down the drive for the last time I wondered? Was it that our diminutive daughters learned to drive in her, barely seeming able to control her large body? Was it that she was our son's mode of transportation when he was coming of age? Was it that our last fairy tale vacation as a family was lived in the confines of her vast interior? (Funny how all the "uglies" drift away in some memories and you are left with a soft fuzzy glow). The vacation when our eldest was 16 and I knew it was the last time we would retreat together, just us. Those sparkling summer days spent surfing in warm water that's meant to be swam in and coming "home" exhausted, napping, lifetime bonds forming, soft voices, nails being painted shades of pink—the last of the summer sun pulling back over the distant mountains—the feeling of deep contentedness and rightness with the world.

Some memories are like that—soft, warm, and sweet. This one was wrapped in an old green suburban.

So long, Curby.

Helping with the Grands

Life is interesting in its newness, and its sameness. As I am with my daughter Sarah, helping with her two Littles I keep thinking of my mom. How she came when I had two of my children. Sister Liz came shortly after I had my second daughter, sister Joanna arrived when Sarah joined the family, sister Carol came when we had Ava and grandma Anita came when our youngest was born. So with each new arrival, we had a close family member who came to welcome the baby and to help the family adjust.

This tradition of older women coming to help young moms with their babies, is such a privilege and honor. Such a blessing all around to everyone. It's a giving and a receiving.

As I am with Sarah and her children, I'm remembering things my mom said and did, and now I am doing the same things. Life continues in its worthy traditions. The young become old, and the rhythm of life goes on, with all the ups and downs, the feelings, thoughts, actions and words. Traditions are passed on with love in action.

It's something to consider, the ebb and flow of life and traditions. How quickly time passes.
Sarah was loving on her children and she asked me, "Did you love us this much?" She continued, "It's hard for me to think these little girls will grow up and leave." It is. Young parents are raising the future generation. Then the young parents will become the older wiser ones who can teach and love by example.

Sometimes it just brings me up short watching these little people. They are so fascinating! I admire the Littles and all the cute and funny things they do. It's so interesting just watching them discover, play and move their little bodies around. God did an amazing job creating humans!! It's a miracle how they are formed and born, how they discover speech and movement... Little by little, line upon line, precept upon precept. One little finger point, then a fist punch, then quick little hands grabbing everything! The drooling "mamamas" eventually turn into words. Scribbles on walls become intricate works of art. It's captivating!

The 2-year-old has full-on conversations; it sounds like a mix of Finnish and Chinese. She knows what she's saying, arm gestures included! Enough words are somewhat legible so we just agree with her. She is life in motion. Go go go. Stands on the table and swings the chandelier, walks on the stone wall behind the house, "washes" dishes and draws beautiful pictures— on every surface!! And the baby just laughs and takes it all in.

This morning big sister handed the baby a blanket, baby clasped her little hands around it, dutifully holding it in her lap. All the while holding the love of her life in her dazzlingly blue gaze. In fact, she loves her mama so much, she wakes up many, many times a night just to visit. Then the toddler wakes up early, and the day begins.

There's stress and harmony, tears and belly laughs. Snuggles and little fingers wrapped around yours. There's splattered food and poopy diapers and laundry and meals to prep and sweeping. There's pool parties and walks in the park and books to read. There's taking turns making pictures in a notebook. There's silly times and sad times. And somehow you find time to get groceries, take a shower, do the dishes and pay the bills.

Life happens. I've heard it said that the days are long but the years are short. Sarah and I were talking about something we saw on social media. By the time a child leaves home, you will have spent 93% of the time that you will ever spend together. That's kind of sobering. It reminds a person, that the daily little things actually are the big things that make up a life.

Time spent together is priceless. Sarah and I talk about sweet things, and we talk about the harder things. Sometimes sad things, sometimes encouraging life-giving things.

And so it goes. Life happens, time marches on. Relationships expand or shrink. Traditions are kept or lost. God is honored, love grows.

I wondered out loud if the children will remember these months I've spent with them. Sarah said, "No, probably not, but I will."

She will. And I will. The cycle of life and love will continue. Prayerfully she will one day be the Gramma who goes to help her precious daughters— being a blessing and being blessed.

Finding Beauty as Winter Sets in

Well, it looks like it's snowing for real now, up here in the Upper Peninsula. It's those teeny tiny flakes that seem to sprinkle on forever.

Since I'm inside, I decided to hunker down and work on my health a little more, so I decided to do a liver cleanse. In the middle of the cleanse, I can only eat hummus and fish, some fruits and veggies. Only clean carbs for a few days, then only veggie carbs. No goodies. Is life worth living with no bread, no mashed potatoes, no fruit/cream-filled jelly roll things I found at the "Nisu" diner in Hancock? I'm just wondering.

I guess those are my comfort foods. So instead, I'm putting a turkey breast going in the crockpot, and sautéing some vegetables with quinoa—funny thing, I'm actually enjoying eating more veggies.

So, when I feel up to it, I continue to dig into closets and chests here at my mother-in-law's. There is a nondescript chest upstairs that I walked by for months as I sorted and cleaned. I finally asked my husband if he had a key for it. He said yes, but you just push the button and it opens... Oh. Silly me.

I pushed the button and it was this beautiful cedar-lined chest full of glorious table linens! I love table linens. I love tea sets, dishes, flowers and all that goes with lunch dining and sweet tea parties.

My husband thought some of these linens were his mother's and grandmother's— some maybe from his paternal grandma's ancestors from Yugoslavia. I can't wait to hear more!

Can you imagine all the effort that went into all of the beautiful creations they made? All the time and energy. . . to make just one fluffy, intricate, beautiful little luxury?

It's interesting to me, how through the ages people always sought beauty. Jars of clay, painted murals in caves, thatched baskets, beaded leather, woven rugs, gold-lined dishes, embroidered cloth.

Some of the descriptions in the Bible are outstanding also. How God told them to make the curtains for the sanctuaries, the gold items, the robes they wore.

I think God put design and beauty in our souls. We long for things of symmetry and pulchritude, or maybe the word is pulchritudinous? (I've always wanted to use that word! Well, since I heard it in a spelling bee.)

Anyway, it makes me wonder what the place Jesus is preparing for us is going to look like! When he left this earth, he said he was going to prepare a place for us. I'm thinking it's probably about done by now.

I am ready for all that Jesus-love, all the people gone on ahead, sitting around that big 'ol feasting table (with a beautiful table covering and fancy dishes), the crystal sea and streets of gold surrounding.

I'm also ready for some supreme mashed potatoes and a cream-filled jelly roll thing! I wonder if they will be on the menu?

Open the Windows, Live in Community and LOVE

Even though it's easier to be alone, we ache for community. Do you feel it? God has wired us this way--He made us in His image--(the triune God exists in perfect union). Do we have "uni-bomber spirituality?" Just me and my Bible and Jesus? Is it too hard to deal with people, so we just don't bother? In the world, there has been a collapse of community and people are suffering. The good news is: *all things are possible through the Spirit working in our lives!* God created us to be connected with others. The early church worked out their differences and dysfunction; they lived in fellowship and common love. The LORD showed them favor and added to the church daily. Many times, Jesus instructed his followers to love one another so that Christian love would draw others in.

Blessings flow when we, as Christians, get along and love one another. When we live in love, it gives off a sweet-smelling savor, a good fragrance that others can note. What flavor is our life giving off? When we open our windows (either personally or collectively), what does the world notice? We were meant to do life together (in love) and to be a witness to the world. There are a lot of people, right now, who are LOST, without Jesus . . .forever. That breaks my heart. I don't know about you, but years ago, I lived a life of desperate sin apart from Jesus. I understand when others act out in sinful ways, their hearts are crying out; they need the love of Jesus! They need US, the believers, to draw them into the family of Christ.

I see a church, a collective body of believers, over-coming our differences, focusing on Jesus and what He has done for us, and together, opening our windows, hearts, and anything else that has been closed off and shut down. I see Jesus standing, his arms are extended. He is drawing us together in love and breaking our hard hearts with his LOVE, so that we transformed by his POWER and are able to be a witness to the LOST right here in our communities. Do you see it?!

Will you join me in asking Jesus to do only what He can do? Are we willing to let Him break our hearts so that the sweet savor of His LOVE and community and joy surrounds us and makes a difference in the world?

Making Deliveries and Remembering Old Times

I was delivering some stuff today, out in the general area where I grew up. I drove down the road that we bumped over every day for many years, picking up kids on the school bus, Tum Tum Mountain looming.

Then I went into the old IP Mill— once a thriving business, now rusting into the ground. But there's an old shed where I had my first real job- weighing log trucks. The shed was much smaller back in the day when I worked there. My dad got me that job; he used to stop by sometime to see how I was doing. That was when I was trying to quit smoking. Ripped up cigarettes in the morning and tried taping them back together in the afternoon. Sitting in the sun, waiting to hear the jake brakes kick in as truckers came sliding onto my scales. That was the summer of '84.

Come fall, I packed up my 18 garbage bags of belongings, said good-bye to the farm folks and headed east with my brother. He was going to New Hampshire for cousin Mark Mattila's wedding, I was going to live with my sister and cousins, to start "really" living- having some FUN!

Well, some of it was fun but, psh. . . seemed like disaster after disaster- starting with driving my brothers pimped-out red Toyota into a badly-placed house in Vermont. . . (it takes talent!) Makes me wonder if I should've just stayed home and weighed log trucks.

That train out at the mill sure was old! The stories it could tell of life and love, tears and joy— and just plain old living. Now it seems like the perfect set for the "Boxcar Children."

I also wondered about the lives of children I used to babysit as I drove by their homes. I remembered being terrified of being left with a croupy baby, and scared at night in a house in the middle or nowhere (listening to the coyotes howl), and babysitting long into the night, then flying home over the prairie in the old green chevy with three on the tree.

Well, these are just some ramblings down memory lane today. Another thing I've been pondering with friends lately is this: back in the day we didn't have as many things to think about, as many things constantly assaulting our minds, clamoring for attention. And I'm beginning to think that's why they're considered the "good old days."

People want peace. Peace of mind, peace in our lives. So thinking about bumping along on a long bus ride, munching on my leftover lunch and watching the world go by my square of window, doesn't really seem like a bad thing after all. And hearing the sound of jake brakes sounds like I'm coming home.

Rivers of Living Water

My brain is straining and groaning with the thought of it! Everyone is doing the best he/she can, in this moment, with what they have . . . and we all need grace. Think about it.

In his or her heart of hearts, no one really wants to be an addict, a yeller, a hater, a manipulator, an angry person. They really don't. We really don't. You. Me. That hurting child inside who is hurting others is crying for help! We all have hang-ups and "work in progress" areas in our lives. Ouch.

Yes, we must set healthy boundaries in our lives. If someone is acting inappropriately, then he or she must own it, not you or me. We need to have those good fences in place, built in love, but there. A healthy boundary that says, "I'm praying for you, but that is your issue, please deal with it. It's not my fault and I'm putting a boundary right here. This is what I'm taking care of (my attitude, my feelings, my issues) and that (on your side of the fence—your attitude, feelings, words, actions, issues) are yours to take care of."

We are doing the best we can right now. I'm working on it. God's not done with me yet. I need grace (absence of judgment, unconditional acceptance). You need grace. Not condemnation. Not shame. Not rejection. Not ridicule. Not gossip. Wouldn't it be a different world, wouldn't we be different people if we really lived grace-filled lives? If we really lived like we "have the mind of Christ?" (1 Cor. 2:16)

So, there's the grace part and there's the truth part. God wants us to set those boundaries, to keep ourselves sane, in Him, and growing. He also wants us (hard as it is) to say those hard things (speaking truth), in love. Things that others may not want to hear. However, when we speak calmly, in love, we are doing as we are called to do. (Eph. 4:15, John 1:14)

LORD! My mind is swimming! Grace, LORD, grace! Fill us up. Let us BELIEVE on YOU as the scriptures say, so that more of YOU would flow out of us like "rivers of living water!" Illumine our eyes so we can see more of you, more grace, more truth, more love! (John 7:38)

Rivers, Lord. I pray for rivers. Rivers of grace-filled living waters. Hallelujah!

Enchanted Childhood

I want to go back to a place of enchanted dreams and childhood memories.

A place of sun-warmed white-washed walls, with paint peeling gently on the edges. This place where sheer white curtains flutter their tattered hems in the breeze of open windows— raised to let in the morning sunshine. This place where the peaceful day waits to unfold with all the sights, sounds, smells and feels of golden youth mixed with aged beauty. A happy place.

This home where blankets have been hastily flung off in anticipation of the waiting day. This era of goodness and grace, that welcomes small feet running down the stairs and out to the lovely day—quickly noting Mother dear frying sausage and whole-wheat pancakes in the cast-iron pan—a smile in her eyes as she acknowledges the child in motion.

A thought flits across my mind—am I the mother or the child in this happy scene? Am I an active participant or an invisible bystander—someone holding the vintage camera, slowly storing these moments in the passage of time.

I notice the child floating off the edge of the wooden porch, feet barely touching the floor. The old screen door squeaks softly, sharply banging shut behind the whirlwind child, all joyful anticipation.

A puff of dust rises with the bang. Bare feet feel the tantalizing pleasure of soft green grass folding underneath, the sun finds the raised face as she runs through the field of wildflowers. Fingers gently tug a few of them as this child of the morning dances along.

Ahead, sisters have laid out an old afghan. Baby dolls are sitting awkwardly along the edge, their too-large clothing bunched together with rubber bands. A basket of dishes bangs against legs as the morning nymph runs awkwardly, but happily toward them.

They will set up the miss-matched plates and cups, mother will bring the breakfast feast and they will enjoy this beautiful time together. This beautiful time together, in this place of happiness and peace. This place of dreams.

Is this real or does it only exist in the enchanted dreams of my childhood, in this home of bygone days, in this field of wildflowers and memories? Or is it like most fond remembrances—a combination of truth, with the passage of time mellowing it into an ethereal montage of sweet beauty and love.

Special Times Growing Up

As I was reading the adventures of "Hank the Cow Dog" to my youngest children, I was remembering some special times growing up on the farm . . .

Dad would read to us on cold winter evenings from the Bible, Luther, Laestadius, Heidi, the Dog of Flanders, or Pilgrim's Progress. He would be exhausted after a full day of morning barn chores and working at his Forest Service job. After supper, Dad and the barn crew would bundle up and finish the outside chores. The rest of us would clean up supper after the usual "avoid the chores and disappear" routine, and then we would gather in the living room to read.

Dad read, Mom would try not to fall asleep while someone combed her hair, and us kids would peel and eat juicy oranges. Did you know the white part of the orange is called pith? We had a lot of fun with that word.

In the summertime, Mom would take us on picnics down the sun-dappled "Shady Lane" to the backfields. She would recite poetry and tell stories. As we got older, the summer months were filled with making hay, library runs, picking produce, canning, canning, and more canning! After the daily work was done, we would jump into the golden yellow suburban and hurtle down to Saddle Dam for a quick dip before complete darkness covered the water. Because if it did, the stumps that were lurking in the depths of the water developed tentacles that would reach up and pull us under. Still gives me the shivers!

In the fall time, we would make wood in the backfield and roast marshmallows over the burn piles. Sometimes Dad would throw some chemicals on the fire that made beautiful colors dance in the flames.

Good memories. Funny, we did work a lot, but that doesn't stick in my mind as a bad thing. It was an essential part of our lives. Made us who we are. . . readers, mothers, fathers, story-tellers, and people who avoid canning (well, that would describe me at least)!

Not a Spirit of Fear

For God hath not given us a spirit of fear, but of power, and love, and a sound mind. (2 Tim 1:7)

We are powerless to change things we are not aware of or do not understand. Do you realize that the source of 80% of our problems are rooted in fear? In the Bible, God tells us not to fear 365 times! He knew it is something with which we would struggle. Fear is called by many names: stress, anxiety, insecurity, panic . . . Fear is unique because it affects the whole person—mind, body, emotions, etc. Fear is the engine that drives self-destructive behaviors. Addictive coping behaviors are ways to temporarily feel normal, self-gratification.

Finding the root of our problems (what is causing our addictions) is the key to change. Once we identify the root, we can begin to untangle the truth from the lies. We can begin to take risks to change in the right direction. We can begin to hope in bright tomorrows. We can walk in grace and truth. God's word speaks truth and life into our hearts. Praise you, Jesus!

You make known to me the path of life;
in your presence there is fullness of joy;
at your right hand are pleasures forevermore.
(Ps 16:11) Adapted from God's word and the "Genesis Process" by Michael Dye

Called to Freedom

For you were called to freedom, brothers. Only do not use your freedom as an opportunity for the flesh, but through love serve one another. For the whole law is fulfilled in one word: "You shall love your neighbor as yourself." But if you bite and devour one another, watch out that you are not consumed by one another.

But I say, walk by the Spirit, and you will not gratify the desires of the flesh. For the desires of the flesh are against the Spirit, and the desires of the Spirit are against the flesh, for these are opposed to each other, to keep you from doing the things you want to do.

But if you are led by the Spirit, you are not under the law. Now the works of the flesh are evident: sexual immorality, impurity, sensuality, idolatry, sorcery, enmity, strife, jealousy, fits of anger, rivalries, dissensions, divisions, envy, drunkenness, orgies, and things like these. I warn you, as I warned you before, that those who do such things will not inherit the kingdom of God.

But the fruit of the Spirit is love, joy, peace, patience, kindness, goodness, faithfulness, gentleness, self-control; against such things there is no law. And those who belong to Christ Jesus have crucified the flesh with its passions and desires.

If we live by the Spirit, let us also keep in step with the Spirit. Let us not become conceited, provoking one another, envying one another.
(Gal. 5:13-26 ESV)

My editing sister reminded me of the following quote by Chief Joseph. I thought it was so good I wanted to add it. She said, "Remember when we were so interested in learning about Indians?" I remember. We even found some arrowheads on our farm growing up. My mom and dad were very sympathetic to the cause of Native Americans, who were grossly mistreated.

"Let me be a free man, free to travel, free to stop, free to work, free to trade where I choose, free to choose my own teachers, free to follow the religion of my fathers, free to talk, think and act for myself—and I will obey every law or submit to the penalty. And I will fight no more forever!"

Early Brain Development and Addictions

"Early childhood brain development can have a direct influence on what you struggle with later in life." (from the "Genesis Process" by Michael Dye)

Awhile back, I journey through the "Genesis Process" that set me free of many sins, fears, and destructive thought patterns. Just another step in the pathway of life. If you are struggling to understand addictions, this will help. The principles in this Process are so profound and fundamental to understanding why we do the things we hate to do (Paul said it, right?). This also speaks to parents in how we respond to the cries of our child—this is brain-building stuff. I just have to share these ideas with you and I hope they bless you, as they are blessing me. Very insightful. Selah!

In the first two years of life, the part of our brains that are developing have to do with our ability to bond, trust, and relate to others. The brain is deciding whether the world is safe or dangerous. Babies depend on others to get their needs met. If a baby cries out and the needs are met in comforting ways, the baby comes to believe that having needs that create vulnerability are a good thing because they result in comfort and reward, i.e., the world is safe. Two things happen: The baby learns to receive gratification from others and the brain becomes creative and free to explore the world.

On the other hand, if the baby is born into a dysfunctional, abusive, or addicted family and the needs are not met, the baby will experience the world as unsafe, creating stress. Having needs makes you vulnerable. When crying out results in abuse or neglect, the brain learns that you have to take care of yourself, resulting in what is called a survival, or hyper-vigilant brain. The brain searches for ways to feel normal or free of stress. If the child cannot bond and trust others, he/she has to learn to gratify self. The brain begins to cut off the neurons that are learning to trust and bond because trying to trust and bond results in pain, fear, and stress. This can be the beginning of what predisposes a person to become attracted to self-gratifying coping behaviors—addictions.

The part of the brain that controls our survival memories and responses is called the limbic system. This system has a separate memory from the conscious part of our brains. It records experiences that have to do with pleasure and reward, hurt, and fear. The limbic system sets up emotional (and behavioral) responses to avoid things that have caused fear and pain and repeats things that have to do with pleasure and reward. This is where coping behaviors come from. When we do something to take away stress (in order to feel normal) the limbic system can associate it with survival and it becomes part of the craving, pleasure, and reward (do it again!) system.

Growing up in a situation that result in a lot of stress, the limbic system becomes like radar, searching for ways to reduce stress and make a person feel normal again. Addictions are not about feeling good or getting high; they are about ways to be free of stress and pain, thus temporarily feeling normal, because normal is associated with survival.

Brain imaging research has identified three areas that this part of the brain is responsible for: food, sex, and safety. These areas produce cravings. Food and sex are obvious, but safety is the area where such things as drugs, alcohol, work, anger, control, relationships, isolation, and religion have been associated with pushing painful unwanted thoughts, feelings, and stressful memories temporarily to the background. In doing so, a temporary sense of safety and peace emerges. Even procrastination, denial, and confusion can become addictions. They reduce the fear and stress of having to change or take action, making us temporarily feel ok. The limbic system can associate these coping behaviors with survival, which can become habitual. The limbic system is part of what the Bible calls the heart.

Whew! That's a lot of info. Good stuff, hey? Lord, help us to learn truth and to be set free. Thank you, Jesus

(Gal. 5:1; James 1:5; Eph. 5:15-17)

In Relationship with the Living God!!!

Being in relationship with the Living God rocks! Sometimes I am completely humbled by His majesty. Sometimes I say, "Woe is me, I am undone." Other times I just seem to admire His Beauty from afar. Then there are times, when He completely sweeps me off my feet and charges me from the inside out! You know what I'm talking about? That "it's gonna be great, it's gonna be wild, and it's gonna be full of Him" kind of moment.

God, you are so incredibly wild and passionate! So full of fire and gentleness. You overwhelm and satisfy me! . . . And the fact that You reach others through us. I can hardly imagine?! You, the Creator of the Universe says we are the salt and the light. You work in and through us.

We welcome you, Holy Spirit! Ignite our fires and let us BURN for YOU and also for the ones who don't yet know you. Yet. Let us be a blessing and an encouragement to those around us. Oh, you are incredible God. We are so thankful to know you in the power of your resurrection! . . . Let that knowledge fuel our passion for you and your kingdom!

Walking with the Living God. Woowee!

(Jer. 29:11; Rev. 3:20; James 4:6-10)

Moving Out

Today the birds are chirping up a storm and the rain is threatening; I'm glad for the bird songs, but I think I'm just gonna have a little cry because I'm a mom and I can do that.

Our youngest moved out last night. Yes, it's part of life and he's going to have a good time hanging out with friends and learning new adulting skills. I'm proud of him and he knows I love him.

He's been a good boy, now he's off to be an awesome man. Thank you, Lord! . . . I haven't looked in his room yet, but I did notice the familiar row of shoes is gone from under the hall table, his essentials are gone from the bathroom and his work boots won't be here waiting for him in the morning anymore.

His car is loud, but he's respectful and didn't "open it up" in the neighborhood very often. Sometimes I would stand outside and listen to him leave, sending a prayer for his safety with the evening breezes. Funny how we do those mom things.

Sometimes, he would come down in the evenings for a back rub when I'd be watching a movie, sometimes he'd watch with me for a while, sometimes not. Sometimes he and his sister would talk in accents and do funny things. I would be laughing in the background, thinking how much joy they bring.

He will still bring joy, but now it will be mostly elsewhere and I will miss this young man of mine and all his quirky funny ways, all these little things.

Like mothers do, I've pondered his comings and goings and his life path for almost 20 years. I wish him all the best in everything! But moms will be moms, and today the love-and-moving-on-tears may continue to splat down my checks and roll off my chin, and that's ok. I have seen his other five siblings leave also; I will make it through.

It's not every day that your youngest leaves the nest—and takes all his shoes and stuff with him! We will feel his absence.

Godspeed, son. Our love and prayers are with you.

Sweet Jesus—Come!

I was thinking about something... Especially at this time of year, it seems that we want to gather with family and friends— to share the wonder of the true meaning of Christmas, and also to enjoy all the hustle and bustle, gifts and food and laughter and love.

But sometimes that doesn't happen. Sometimes our best-laid plans go awry, due to weather or other circumstances and we are unable to gather as we want. Sometimes we may feel left out and home alone. Sometimes our world seems bleak, without much light or hope. Finances may be low, children may be sick, relationships broken, things may not be going as planned.

Then I started thinking about Mary—knowing she was carrying the baby Jesus, looking for somewhere to give birth.

Being told time and again that there was "no room for them in the inn."

Clambering back on the donkey and clumping along, pregnant belly jostling side-to-side, hurting.

Her water may have broken, maybe running down her leg. Hurry Joseph, hurry. Where oh where, to lay down and give birth?!

Then Joseph may have spotted the low stable, a cave in the hillside. He looked at Mary with a questioning gaze. Her face was contorted in pain.

She nodded. The tears flowed. "This wasn't how I imagined this special child to come! I wanted the comforts of home; I wanted my mother and my sisters by my side. I wanted someone to hold my hand and wash my baby."

But that wasn't how things went.

There was a dirty stable. A stone manger. Some animals, maybe some hay and the smell of manure.

Then Jesus came into the world... and everything changed.

A hillside lit up with the light from a host of angels singing and praising God! The watching shepherds, the lowest people in society, were led to the stable to worship the baby, the chosen one... the messiah.

Mary watched them in awe, kneeling at the manger to see what God had done. Faces shone! Her gaze lifted above the smelly stable, tears flowed, her heart sang.

Jesus had come and everything had changed.

May the same be true for each of us this Christmas season. May our gazes be lifted to the heavens. May we SEE Jesus!! May our hearts be light and our countenances happy—no matter our earthly circumstances.

May Jesus come to each of us—sweet Jesus—He changes everything. Hallelujah!

Emotional Intelligence

Have you read Daniel Goleman's book, "Emotional Intelligence?" If not, I would definitely suggest it. It is so easy to read and it holds incredible truths that will increase our level of understanding in our relationships with others. I deeply appreciated the discussion on empathy; it made so much sense. If a person can pick up and translate the non-verbal emotions of others, they are empathetic. If a person is not attuned to his or her own emotions, they cannot do this; they seem out of touch with others.

I have always believed self-awareness is important; this discussion on empathy reinforces that belief, in that empathy builds on being self-aware. That empathy then translates into being able to feel another's pain as if it were our own. Furthermore, the roots of morality are in empathy—if a person is able to identify a potential victim, it is in sharing their distress, that we are forced to act. It then makes perfect sense that the person who is lacking in empathy is able to molest or otherwise harm others.

I am thankful that prison psychologists are working with inmates to increase their empathy; it gives hope that empathy can be taught and learned. This is such an important life-skill; I am thankful schools are embracing more measures to help children increase compassion. It is also something that should be taught and modeled in the home, along with discussions on appropriate ways to acknowledge personal feelings and those expressed by others.

Very sobering is the discussion on psychopaths—those who are incapable of feeling empathy or compassion at all; they are unable to emotionally connect with others.

"Emotional Intelligence" by Daniel Goleman is such a helpful tool; I love it! I appreciate how he brings forth truthful concepts, gives a scenario, and then backs up what he presents with studies and expert accounts.

Google it!

Times change, people change, circumstances change. But these two things remain: God is faithful and you can Google anything. I know, not really on the same page at all, but for me, awhile back, they were.

Feeling frustrated and out of sorts with us not finding exactly the right place to move to, I typed a prayer into the Google search bar: "Where are we going to live, Lord?" And this is what popped up: "WE ARE GOING TO LIVE IN HEAVEN says the Lord Jesus Christ."

My eyes nearly popped out of my head! So cool! And it continued, "Do not let your hearts be troubled. Trust in God, trust also in me." It referenced John 14, so I looked it up. It is a beautiful chapter, filled with encouragement.

Thank you, Lord, for reminding me where I'm going, where we will live, what your plans are for my life, and for reminding me our hope and trust is secure in your eternal truths.

P.S. In our Father's house are many rooms—custom-built for each of us by Jesus the carpenter. Don't you just love that? Lord, I am humbled once again by your majestic servant heart.

Parenting—Well Done!

As a parent, I have learned a few things by watching others. I have learned a few things by reading books, learning in classrooms, and from my kids. And I have learned a few things in the school of hard knocks—hard knocks on a hard block!

Parenting is one the hardest and most rewarding things we will ever do in life. If you are a parent, I am sure you will agree. The joys of seeing the first smile, the first step, the first (and every one in between!) graduation makes the heart swell to bursting. The sorrow of experiencing the first frown, the first wrong step, the first orientation into a wrong choice shrinks the heart to breaking. And so it is with parenting—joys and sorrows. Sorrow and joy.

As a parent, the time is short and we do not get too many chances to get things right, do we? However, I am thankful for grace, for re-dos, for being able to go back to my kids and say, "I made a mistake, I did it wrong, can you forgive me?" There is incredible power and healing there—on so many levels. In doing so, we clear our conscious, our mind, and open spaces for better learning. We also set an example to our watching children.

Through the years, I have read many books on communication, relationship, and parenting; I have been learning as I go, as I'm sure you have too. I have had to ask myself, "What am I doing and why am I doing it" numerous times. Really. Why am I insisting on this course of action, this way of doing something? Is it best for me, or best for my child? Do they really need to be potty-trained before two? Do they really need to wear the red coat with the black shoes? Color in the lines?

A good leader asks, "What do you need from me and how can I help you meet your goals?"

We would do well to consider the same as we parent. What does this child need from me and how can I bring him/her up, guiding them in the way they should go?

Sometimes we look at confrontation with our children as a bad thing, but is it really? Do we really need to get our kids back into line, browbeat them into submission, control them? God help us. I am trying to think of a time when God treated me that way, and I am coming up with a blank. Nada. None.

So, why did I treat my kids that way at times? Why indeed? Why do any of us? God help us.

Bad behavior is caused by un-met needs, so we must ask, "What does this child truly need? "Or is the "bad behavior" simply a reflection of my own expectations, my own lack of skills, and not a reflection on the child's behavior at all?

Given that the human brain does not develop fully until well into the 20s, our children lack the reasoning, weighing, and considering skills we possess. It is our job to model to them how that happens—hmmm, if I make this choice, this happens, or if I make that choice, that would be the consequence. Hmmm, that's a big decision, let's weigh the pros and cons. You see?

Sometimes, we expect our toddlers to have these skills when the wires in the gray matter simply have not yet been connected.

As a gramma and mother for 34 years now, I now say, "If we err, let's err on the side of grace." Let's assume the best, train in the way they should go, model these higher-level thinking skills, and let nature/God work out the rest.

Too many times as parents, we do the old "knee jerk" thing. We respond out of our lack of skills, sleep, etc. It would do us well to make sure we are functioning as well as possible because the task of parenting is not for the faint of heart. We must take care of ourselves—mind, body, and spirit. We must be nurtured and fed and watered and rested if we are to parent well.

Some of us come from the era when shame and blame were the name of the game. "Who dunnit," "shame on you," and "bad, bad boy" were how things rolled. Time has shown us where those kinds of ideas have left us filled with shame, guilt, anger, and addictions.

Experience, education, and an encounter with the Divine have led me to a very different place.

If we err, let's err on the side of grace. The fruits of a good spirit—patience, kindness, and gentleness are how the Divine say we must act. The rest of it—shame, blame, and harshness can go back to the pit from where they came—they have no place in a home that is built on truth and grace.

We live and learn, God help us.

When I got some good spiritual and natural teaching, things started to make sense to me and the craziness in my brain and life has been replaced by a deep sense of rightness and peace, and I am thankful. I have gained some clarity and insight. Thank God.

We can do this, friends. Parenting is one the hardest and one the best things we will ever do. Let's do it well. We have the tools. Let's equip ourselves, let's be steeped in grace and truth.

Let's take on a mantle of grace, of learning, of working things out together. Let's take a look at some ideas that might make us a little uncomfortable, let's dig for nuggets of truth. Let's mine for the vein of gold and follow it.

Do you know that those who have a sense of well-being and success in living are those who have the courage to do well and succeed? Courage is paramount to success. So how do we get courage?

We foster a sense of courage when we provide safe places, places where the heart can rest and the soul can soar and the mind can think—where people know they belong.

We foster a sense of courage when we encourage with kindness, offer reproof with gentleness, and patiently model good behavior.

We foster a sense of courage when our demeanor is in tune with the Creator and we radiate love and peace and joy. So, if you have been struggling with "how in the world do I make sense of this" and "how am I ever going to get it right," go back to the Source. Seek truth and grace, life and light.

And you will find it.

We can do this. Take heart.

Parenting is one the hardest things we will ever do, but we are not alone and there is incredible JOY on the journey. The first reconciliation, the first lesson learned, the first "thank you" makes it all worthwhile. For some, it is looking forward to the first reunion on the far side of glory—and glorious it will be!

The rewards are great. The hard work pays off.

We all cherish those words—well done, well done!

So, let's live it—well done.

Cognitions become Behaviors. . . Hmmm

Cognitions: definition - the mental faculty or process of acquiring knowledge by the use of reasoning, intuition, or perception.

What kind of cognitions/thoughts chase each other around in your brain all day? Positive? Hopeful? Sad? Condemning? Because what we think determines how we feel and how we feel, determines how we act and interact. So, can you honestly say the statements at the end of this note? How about your kids? Do they believe they are competent? Are they confident in whom God made them to be and the abilities they have? God made us all in His image—Imagio Deo.

I believe one of the definitions of having the "faith of a child" is trusting in something bigger than ourselves, without having to work at it. Another piece to this is our view of God. If we believe positive things about God—that He is worthy, loving, trustworthy, kind, etc.—that also impacts how we feel about ourselves and our world. But, unfortunately for most of us, the world has beaten that childlike faith out of us; we may no longer think we are worthy or lovable or strong or that we belong . . . and that makes us feel bad and act bad. :(

It serves no one, except the devil for us to feel unworthy. Our deepest human need is to feel loved and accepted. God created us to live in community. We want to feel worthy, loved, and have a sense of belonging. All of us do. And if we don't, then negative thoughts, feelings, and actions follow.

So, until positive affirmations becomes part of our unconscious cognitive thoughts, we must work at regaining that with which we were born— (childlike faith that embraces positive thoughts about ourselves and our world and our God) . . . So, read these statements over and see where your fence is low (or do it with your kids). And then you can work on discovering what you can do to bring thoughts back to a positive frame of mind, which will positively influence how we feel and interact with the world. :) Sometimes just continually repeated truths make them a reality in our minds. We can do all things through Christ.

Believe the positive messages God says about you and all people. It will change everything! Be blessed.

I deserve love. I can have love. I am worthy/worthwhile.
I am loving and lovable. I am fine/attractive/lovable. I can have love.
I am intelligent and able to learn. I am OK just the way I am. I do the best I can. I am competent.
I can learn to trust myself. I can choose whom to trust.
I can safely feel and show my emotions. I can choose to let it out. I am now in control.
I am strong. I now have choices.
I can succeed. I can handle it. I can be myself/make mistakes.
I love myself.
I can love others.

Arriving in Chassell, Michigan

Oh wow!!!! In and around Chassell, Michigan is just lovely too!! This world is beautiful!

It's been so fun visiting with peeps, swimming at Agate Beach on the shore of Lake Superior, gathering rocks, bumming around, and yes! —I found an organic lotus energy drink at a coffee shop!!

It's great being here after many years. Gregg and his people are here and lots of my friends and rellies too. Looking forward to seeing them all. Today I drove by Gramma O's house (it's been remodeled), and my dad's Uncle Art and Ann's home. They're all gone... lots of peeps are passing on, heaven is filling up.

Also, there are tons of lovely birch trees growing native here. Kinda funny, years ago I painted my MIL a picture that featured birch trees. I found it again-hanging on her wall. Mom loved birch trees too; she planted some in the middle of the yard on the farm in Washington.

I'm looking forward to seeing everyone here, digging into my family's history. I'm also looking forward to touring around and learning a bit more of the history of the area— including mining, about those funky large red bricks on older buildings, and comparing all the pasties.

New England Style and History

Driving through New England, I noticed certain similarities between the old houses and towns. I did some research and found some interesting facts.

The typical New England connected farm complex consists of the "big house," which acts as the standard family living quarters. Connected to the "big house" is the "little house," which contains the kitchen area. Next to it is the "back house," which was traditionally a carriage or wagon house. Connected to the back house is a standard livestock barn.

In 1779, the Town of Hancock was incorporated without a designated center. Although named for John Hancock, signer of the Declaration of Independence (who happened to own nearly a thousand acres within the town boundaries), there is no evidence that Governor Hancock ever visited or benefitted the community in any way.

This is the town my husband and I first lived in when we got married. It was an interesting historic place, with all of your typical New England style things—town square, central church, small store, garage, cemetery and fascinating homes. It also had a lake where people boated and swam; one year we watched the fireworks bursting over the water there.

These small towns were first settled by Puritans, Scotch, English and Irish, bringing their various cultures together. They cleared land and prepared ground for crops. Many of them fervently wanted to build a meeting house, place to worship the Lord. These early settlers were extremely poor, but they built a church meeting place and called their first preacher to duty. The old church no longer remains. I found it interesting that people owned their pews in the main seating section, and also in the balcony. They also designated an area to bury their dead. In 1819 their first church structure was burned to the ground. A new church was built, at this point people had a bit more wealth. In 1851 the church was moved, updated and stands there today. The carriage stalls also still stand behind the church.

Almost every building on Main Street in downtown Hancock is listed on the National Register of Historic Places as part of the Hancock Village Historic District. Hancock's Meetinghouse is home to Paul Revere's #236 bell, which chimes on the hour, day and night. The town does not have paved sidewalks, but gravel paths leading from home to home.

In 1623 Hancock was mostly a fishing and trading post and remained so until about 1760 when various entities made bids on the land. In 1879 Hancock held their first centennial celebration. The program was full of scripture reading and singing and prayers.

What's your John Hancock? Have you ever wondered where that saying came from? As president of the Continental Congress, John Hancock's signature was the first to be affixed to the Declaration of Independence.

Not sure of their position in the world, the towns and colonies were detaching from Great Britain; not quite states, the colonies searched for titles in calling their first meeting. "Town meetings delivered to town government what primary schools are to science says de Tocqueville. They bring it within the peoples' reach; they teach men how to use and enjoy it."

In the towns, the colonies were developing a race of men who knew their rights, and in knowing, they dared maintain them. When our forefathers came together in a town meeting, they were putting into practice the lessons they had learned in the various towns, where they were born and educated.

God's Character – My Identity – My Attitude

But now, thus say the LORD, your Creator, O ___(your name)_____ , and He who formed you, O ____(your name)_____, Do not fear; for I have redeemed you; I have called you by name; you are Mine! (Is. 43:1)

As we think, so we are. (Prov. 23:7). As we THINK, so we are. Hmmm, pretty powerful, huh?

What do you think of yourself? What are your thoughts toward yourself? Loser? More than Over-comer in Christ? Or over-the-top?

Because of God's character, we can trust Him. Only in our Creator, can we discover all we are made to become! Our identity is based on who God is and how He chooses to relate to us. These true and correct identity thoughts will produce healthy attitudes that lead to right actions! (Taken from "Gripped by the Greatness of God" by James McDonald.)

God's Character=>	My Identity => My Attitude
God is personal=>	I am chosen => I can be confident
God is present =>	I am strong => I can persevere

God is loving => I am valued => I can have security

God is faithful => I am heard => I can have peace

God is patient => I am forgiven => I can have praise

From Michigan to New Hampshire, Pennsylvania, and back to Michigan

I had the best trip to New Hampshire in 2023. I had so much fun with my funny fun sweet sister, Carol, and my aunt and uncle and cousins and more friends. Carol and I spent as much time together as possible, traipsing around visiting and going to thrift stores and out for breakfast, exploring and swimming (we love to go swimming!) and a day trip to Wilmington, Vermont—that was so special! It was charming and sweet, full of fun and laughter. We went to the coast with our cousin and we enjoyed the day so much! Lois is such a pal, going back to childhood. Oh, and scrunching along in the soft sand!! I had so much fun with all the people there, including my friend Connie, who so graciously let me stay with her—so much hospitality. I reconnected with cousins and friends that I had not seen for ages. It made my heart squeeze in all the right places.

I spent the summer swimming in Lake Superior – I loved it so much!! So the lakes in New Hampshire were like bathwater...Sunshine Lake or Gilmore Pond and the loons called to me every day while I was there :-) But Lake Superior is something else. Huge and cold! She surrounds the Upper Peninsula of Michigan, so there are many places to swim—and each is quite different. It's been lovely exploring them all.

Then I went down to Mennonite country for a while and stayed at a working dairy farm. The people and the children and kitties and everything was so sweet and beautiful. Met some new and old friends – quite fascinating … God is everywhere. The clackety-clack of the horses and buggies sang to me! I was able to experience a town festival there with the Mennonites and other town folks at an old iron stone-built forge.

Funny thing-I asked the young gal who was putting food orders together if the burger or the chicken sandwich was better. She said definitely the chicken. So I said, "OK, I will get that please." And she put it in a bag. Later, when I went to eat my chicken burger, I pulled out a chicken leg! One whole big leg. So I messily gnawed on that for a while. Pretty good actually, but not my preferred way to eat chicken! But all of it there in Pennsylvania touched my heart—such a sweet satisfying way to live.

I also went to the Sight and Sound theater in Lancaster County and saw the Moses production. Epic! —huge screens and live actors and animals. I sat by Ruth and Hannah, more lovely souls wearing little white caps. They bought me candied almonds.

I stopped at a beautiful town called Little Falls in New York. Wow!! That was so picturesque, tucked into a hillside – so much history, and thinking about all the people coming here from abroad to make a better life. I also saw part of the Erie Canal there :-)! I remembered the song my mom taught us, "Get up there Sal, you're past that barge, 15 miles on the Eire Canal!"

Then I stopped in Frankenmuth Michigan, It's a little Austrian town. That was also quite lovely, beyond lovely! There is so much good yet in America. I love chatting to people and hearing their stories along the way :-). I also saw lots of rolling hills and farms and nice barns and sweet homes. Many gorgeous (and some humble) churches. . . Hallelujah! hopefully we fill them up, praising the LORD.

Well, that's been part of my journey. Getting to Michigan from Washington and all my adventures here is another story!

God bless you all on your journey!! He wants us to connect and do life together. I hope you find joy in the moments. I'm back in the UP of Michigan for a while yet. God knows. It's beautiful here this time of year.

"Let the words of my mouth and the meditation of my heart be acceptable in thy sight, oh Lord my strength and my redeemer."

Yard Sale: Summer Combat

If you are planning to hold a yard sale, do not make the mistake that I did and think you will sell some decent stuff at a fair price, without having a haggle on your hands for every quarter you make. Maybe it was the time of year—July sales in my home town bring hardened dealers looking for excellent merchandise at give-away prices. On the other hand, holding a sale in April is a much better chance to actually sell your stuff without a knockdown, drag-out for each dollar you make. At that time of year, the miscreants are just aching to get out of the house and having the pleasure of spending time at your event. They pay what you ask, smile while doing it, and bid you a good day when they leave.

But, back to my July sale. Maybe the problem was in my mind-set. I should have just thought of it as a "Charity Event" and then we all would have been happy. I should have put out flyers that said: "Come to my "sale" (wink, wink), take what you want, pay what you want, use my bathroom, try things on, point out every teeny spot you see, take two for 50 cents (even if the basket is clearly marked 50 cents *each)*, hey, knock yourself out, take three for 10 cents! It is all about you! I want you to leave feeling special and cared for."

Let's meet a few of my customers. First, there was the "grandpa" who wants to buy my daughter's pink, sparkly, practically brand-new bike for half the price. He opens his mouth and I immediately hear "dealer-speak." My hackles rise. These are the people who come to your sale, get the best stuff at bargain-basement prices, gloat as they leave, and put them for re-sale in a shop somewhere. So, after, negotiating for awhile, grandpa ends up paying a fraction of what the bike is worth; saying how his "grand-daughter" needs a new bike. Well, if she exists, I wish her many long, happy hours riding her sweet bike from her generous grand-pop.

Right then, I should have realized I was not practicing the number one rule of selling—detachment. If you are at all attached to something, you should not even think of putting it in your sale. Too many problems arise if you do.

However, if you are like me, once you begin going through your house looking for things to sell, the greed takes over. The smell of money and lust for the sell are the driving forces. If something is not a family heirloom of at least three generations, or an item one of my kids handmade for me, then it's up for sale.

I was also having difficulty in another area. I knew something was a little wrong with my thinking when an older gentleman shuffled up the drive, and asked if this was the place that was selling a rifle. I quickly wondered if he would settle for a BB gun or maybe I could run in the house, call my husband and ask if he had a gun he wanted to get rid of. I dismissed that thought as quickly as it came into my mind; my husband doesn't sell ANY of his stuff. And, he would probably have thought I had spent a little too much time in the sun if I had actually made that call!

Another lady wanted to use my bathroom, try things on, and pay 50 cents for a two-dollar item. She flashed those shiny quarters and I couldn't resist. Then there was the woman who wanted dress-up items that were clearly marked 50 cent *each,* at a price of 50 cents for two because "they were a set." Silly me, I should have offered her the whole bin "just for fun." Oh, and the shopper who ripped the comforter out of the neatly zipped bag, inspected every inch, and offered a third of the price! "Hey lady, you don't have to pay at all, let me carry it to your brand-new car, okay?"

I should take a few tips from my eight-year-old son. Maybe it was the cute fedora he was wearing or maybe it was just his age, or maybe the confidence in what he was selling. Clearly, he had detached; there was no agonizing going on as he deftly handled one customer after another. He named his price (twice what I thought was fair) and people gladly paid it! When someone was trying on a helmet, he brought two more that might work as well. He got kids to pay fifty cents or a dollar for cheap plastic guns. He tried to ask double for some of his items in the dress-up bin, until the wily customer pointed to the price on the tag. He even tried to get me to pay him twice—he pocketed a quarter from the customer and then told me to write it down on the tally sheet! It was an honest eight-year-old mistake. One lady said, "I'll pay his price; he values his stuff."

Huh? I value my stuff.

Next time, I think I will hire a team of veteran eight-year-old yard-salesmen, then I can sit back and say "bring it on; talk to the man in the hat." My days of combat yard sale-ing are over.

On the Road Again

Another beautiful day in the neighborhood! . . . Happy Lords Day. Well, I'm on the road again . . . Heading back to Vancouver for a bit, then on to Tennessee for a nephew's wedding.

Life is rich and full— Not perfect, but my cup does run over. Thank you, Lord.

I know I'll miss my daughter Sarah's sweet family, but I will be back :-)… Interestingly, these old brown hills of the Tri-Cities have grown on me, along with the brilliant sunshine! -yes! And I have to say, I love these road trips with my girl Lauren (Daigle), my boys CCR, the boys of Summer with a little Adele and some Willie thrown in.

It's been so fun to explore new little places and see new sights and feel the presence of God all around. Glorious! . . . On to my favorite coffee shop (or energy drink) I'm stopping at in Goldendale :-)

Now there's an app I should develop – best coffee shops from coast to coast . . .I'm on it! Have a beautiful day!

Ponds and Kids and Living Things

There's something about ponds, kids, frogs, ducks and snakes in the cattails.

After biking and walking down to the pond in the neighborhood, it was fun watching the grandkids throw rocks to make the frogs' bulging eyes disappear into the depths of the murky water. They spotted the ducks and ran around the pond to get a closer look. Of course, the ducks went squawking away, skimming across the slimy water.

We thought it would be wonderful if a big bucket loader could clean out all the sludge in the pond and we could jump in for a little swim. But we knew the bottom would be ooey and gooey, squishy and slimy, so we stayed on the bank.

The cattails were bursting open and spreading their fluff, among all the scratchy grasses. The sky was brilliant blue. The sun blazed. Someone spotted another pond, that had previously lay hidden in tall grass.

We rustled through the brush to get a better look.

The eldest spotted a yellow, orange and red snake in the grass. He thought it would be a good idea for his sisters to stomp on one edge of the patch of grass and make the snake come out on the other side. They turned the challenge around to him, which he of course declined.

Once again they went down and walked out on the culverts to get a better look at frogs doing what frogs do in the green pond.

There's something about poking along the bank of a body of water that entices us as humans. Whether it's the ocean, a lake or river, a little stream or a slimy pond, we are drawn in for a closer look—a poke about in the dirt or sand.

We search for creatures, shells, rocks. We gather these things, bringing them home in buckets, glass jars or soggy pockets. We rinse them off, and dry them, we put them on the shelf.

Sometimes we later pick them up and remember good times along the water's edge. We remember the people who shared those times with us. We remember the jumping frogs, the squawking ducks and the shiny snake in the grass.

This is life at the water's edge in America. This is children at play, adults along for the ride—building memories, growing bonds that draw us closer to the earth and closer to each other.

These are the simple things that, in years to come, we'll remember. We'll remember the brilliant October day that we peddled to the pond. We'll remember smiling into the sun and teasing each other, rustling through the grass.

I looked into their sweet, hot faces and saw peace and the thrill of discovery in their eyes. I saw the slight breeze lift their hair. The air seemed to swell with contentment and love. One of them said we should always live here and come to this special place again. We were happy spending time together where the frogs lurked just under the surface of the still water.

These are things that build a life. The small things that grow a child, which end up being the big things that connect us, one to another.

Clean Sheets

As I flipped the clean sheets out and spread them on the bed in the quiet of the house, it reminded me of all the other times I had prepared for her arrival. My mother-in-law was coming, a child was giving up his bed, the room had been cleaned and made ready.

I spread the sheets and noticed they were quite wrinkled. I'm not sure why—but I felt a need to iron those sheets. You must know, I iron as little as possible. But it felt wrong somehow to put wrinkly sheets on her bed. She would have ironed them for me; back in the day, people ironed everything. They set aside a day for ironing. I plugged in the iron and waited for it to steam. Being a little lazy, I left the sheets on the bed and ironed away. They looked nice and soft, inviting.

She likes a blanket that has a little weight, something that is not too warm. I dug out a lovely vintage quilt and smoothed it on the bed. (Many people from around the world have slept under that quilt.) I realized I missed having overnight guests. There is much to be said for sleeping under the same roof, sharing morning coffee, and late-night rodeos with kids and grandkids.

All the preparations—bed, basket of goodies, nightstand with lamp, clock, and a fan from my mother's—felt like a homecoming preparation. It also reminded me of a book I have read to the kids for years—Nana Upstairs and Nana Downstairs. Nana upstairs is the old white-haired lady, visited by her great-grandson now and then, and soon she dies. Nana Downstairs bustles around and helps the family. Now my mother-in-law is Nana Upstairs and I'm Nana Downstairs. Makes a person think. We've been doing this for 24 years—spending time in each others' houses—but one day, Nana Upstairs will be gone. And time will move on. Makes me want to relish the moments. Iron the sheets. Use the beautiful quilt. Fill the basket with goodies.

The brevity of life. One day I, too, will have white hair and be visited upstairs by my great-grandson.

Life passes. It's been a few years since I wrote the above. We've moved and our children all have places of their own. And unfortunately, my mother-in-law is gone now too. We miss her. I'm thankful for all our good times together and I wish there could have been more.

The Night-Visiting Cat

I need your help to figure something out! Awhile back, I was sleeping and I felt a warm body—actually a warm cat! squirming around in my blanket by my legs, creeping up my body. I tried to wiggle away from it but soon I felt its tail around my neck.

Next thing I know, as I tried to decipher if this was my daughter's gray cat or if it's my mother-in-law's not-too-friendly cat, who is squirming in on me. Eeek! I feel its teeth on my finger! It definitely felt like cat teeth on my finger and I started praying. Oh no... I didn't want it to bite me because one of my friends recently had to go to the hospital twice because she had such a bad infection from her cat biting her.

Soon the feral visitor released its hold on my finger and I was so relieved. I continued to try to squirm away from it because honestly, I don't like cats in the bed with me and I was worried it might sink its sharp claws into me!

After I became completely conscious, I wondered if it was real or part of a dream because here's the thing. My mother-in-law had a big golden cat who lived mostly in the basement. It was not seen by very many people besides her. One night I saw the orange fur ball slinking around the corner and I was terrified that it would attack me, but it just gave a strange howl and leapt down the stairs, leaving a clump of fur behind.

Well, we knew that we'd have to rehome it after my MIL passed, so my husband got a cat trap and was transferring the cat to another trap to bring it to the Humane Society and she escaped!!

Now I'm wondering if she found her way back into the house or if it was all a furry figment of my frightened imagination? But it seemed so real, even down to its pointy little teeth on my finger. I checked for teeth marks, but I didn't see any...???

I better go check the bed for any left-behind cat hair... I had joked that the cat might come back to haunt us... eek! What do you think?

The 40th Psalm

I love how God's word and his mercies are fresh and new every morning! Today I turned to the 40th Psalm for encouragement and meditation; I was filled to overflowing with God's provision! May you be blessed also. . .

He delivers us out of the pit, sets our feet on solid ground and puts a new song into our mouths! A song of praise. We turn away from false gods and begin to see the numerous wonders He has created! He opens our ears to hear what He is speaking to us; we see that He has written about US in His scrolls.

We speak of you and your wonders LORD; we are not silent. We tell of your love, righteousness, faithfulness, and your salvation. Trouble and sin surround us, but we turn to you, oh God. May all who seek to shame us and point fingers at us be "appalled in their shame." (that's what the word says! God does not delight in shaming or finger pointing). But we rejoice in your name and say, "The Lord be exalted!" You are our help and deliverer, do not delay. . .

Thank you, Lord Jesus for your faithful words of truth. Thank you for the encouragement and fresh mercies every day!

(Psalm 40)

Beach: Dissonance and Symphony

I'm on the beach. It's cool now. The surf is beautiful, the sounds mesmerizing, cool breeze, airplanes humming.

Soft sand. Fuzzy blanket to my chin, sitting by a sheltering log. Beach grasses dance. Birds skim the water, clouds puff.

I have been enjoying reading "1000 Gifts" again—about reflective thankfulness. Our contentedness in life, is about what we hear, see and focus on – the clanging noise, the dissonance... or the harmony, the joy. Both have meaning, purpose. There's a time for all things.

When we see and hear the ugly, it ignites compassion, empowers action, change. When we hear the symphony, the heart soars, joy bounds, hope springs.

We want the symphony— but . . . life happens with all of its imperfections. What will be my focus? Where will my heart land? Windows reflect the passing of day. Dark figures move in the distance, scissor-legs, arms swing, a light offshore.

Seagull lands. Head swivels, feathers ruffle. People move: all different shapes, sizes and gaits – young and old – walking, running, skipping through the sand. And I wondered – were they hearing the dissonance or the symphony?

Without the dissonance, the symphony would lose meaning, height, depth.

The sun breaks through the restraint of the clouds. My pen forms a shadow. I watch the ripples in the sand. A beautiful pattern became evident, it was always there. But without the light, I could not see.

Reflection, pure and glorious. It was not lost on me. The cloudscape became 3-D. White gold cotton floating in space, filled with the pungent smell of the sea symphony.

Glory! For me? God, you are too good! This was what I wanted. This is why I came. You restore my soul.

The light and splendor were there for a brief moment, then gone. A large, dark form obscured the light. Dissonance threatened. and then...!

Backlit majesty – the clouds glowed! Fire streaked the sky, distant rays shot heavenward. Who Lord is like you?!

The ebb and flow, light and dark. dissonance and symphony.

Both held tenuously. Both a central part of life's swirling experiences that engage the heart and mind.

Sharing Truths with Teens

For a few years, I went into classrooms for AWARE and shared truth with teens. One year, I talked with 1200 kids about future goals and healthy relationship choices—empowering them with truth. Kids want/need to know this stuff. When kids know the truth, they can be empowered to make the decisions to protect the future they want. Many kids do not even realize it is an option to wait for sex. Other kids never planned to have sex, yet it "just happened." Ever wonder what the number one reason teens have sex? To feel loved. What is the best way to avoid intercourse in a non-married relationship? Avoid arousal. For him, arousal usually begins at French kissing, for her it's sexual touch. That's the truth. Be empowered. Live free in Christ. He has good plans for you! These kids' comments tell the story:

What I learned is you only need to go as far as spending time with someone to get to know them well.

It taught me a lot about what having sex as a kid does to affect you and your future partner.

I learned that any sexual activity that we do can affect our future lives and goals that we have. I think it is very important to know that so it helps us decide to wait or not, like for me, I would wait until I am married. I thought it was an interesting presentation. Thanks.

I liked the intimacy level chart. I learned how even if you have just been with 2 people you could be exposed to multiple STIs.

I liked how much info it gave me and that the person presenting didn't just say "everything is bad, if you do this your stupid" because a lot of people have gone through it.

I have learned about having a good nonsexual relationship. Also that you should save yourself for the person you absolutely love and after you guys get married.

One thing I really learned is that I need to set boundaries in my future relationships so that I don't make horrible mistakes. I should know that if my future girlfriend really does care about me and loves me, she would respect my feelings and want to help me with things.

Pictures in my Heart

As humans, we continually look for meaning in life; we try to make sense of what is happening in and around us.

We gather note-worthy information and then process and file it in memorable places. We seek to gain pleasure and we want to minimize pain—for ourselves, and others. We desire to feel love and a sense of belonging. And in the end, we want to know that our life mattered, that it held connection and deep meaning.

All of those ideals came together for me, un-announced and without warning this past weekend. As the moments happened, I found myself struggling with waves of deep emotions that threatened to overwhelm. And as a well-trained Finn, I was at a loss for words to express.

I wanted to note, process, and file that wonderful weekend. I attempted to gather the ethereal moments that were making up life—our life. I wanted to write the thousands of words that the pictures told. I struggled to capture the monumental memories for safekeeping before they sailed to eternity or we sailed into the next day, the next adventure.

It all started Thursday night. A quick visit with some of the family at mom's—remembering dad's birthday and the good times growing up on the farm. . . Thanksgiving feasts, clear frosty mornings, hungry hunters stopping in for mom's tasty food or giving a toot as they sailed by on the road, eager to set up deer camp.

Then Caitlin and Jesse text, "Can we come for the weekend?" Uh, yeah! Super sweet! Can't wait to get my hands on that fat little grandson and greet his parents. :)

Friday morning hustling around cleaning, then off for a full day of work, collecting Ava from home and charging over to Summit View to help put 170 lunches together for the kids and adults who were heading out into the community on a work day. Beautiful day, thankful to be alive. Thankful to be part of something bigger.

Flying home, finishing laundry (grateful for kids who help!), cleaning, and grocery shopping. Late arrival of Caitlin and family after a grueling drive. Thankful they made it safely; God is good. . . Early morning rising—breakfast of bacon (mmm) and French toast. Banana bread with chocolate chips, requested by Caitlin, baking in the oven. Smells yummy.

Off to the church to drop off Ava (and friend who came home last night) for the day. Beautiful sunrise, sparkling chilly crystals. "Feels like Christmas" my backseat riders say. Mmm-hmm.

More groceries and back home to visit. Get hamburger and sauce bubbling in crock-pot for noon spaghetti. Caitlin and I do a quick stop at Posh and Tattered. Visit with friend. :) God is good. . . Whip up alfredo sauce, cook biscuits and noodles, make salad. Voila!—lunch. Everyone else heads up to my daughter's place (daughter and son-in-law) to help put in their wood stove. Bring a loaf of banana bread. I take a nap. :) God is good. . .

Then I'm off to the church. Cook 40 pounds of beef for tacos. Help in the kitchen, enjoy the camaraderie, meet some new friends, visit with the kids. God is good. Exhausted. Movie and visiting back at home. Good rest. Love my bed. Pre-dawn rising; I remember mom. Always whipping up something delicious in the kitchen. We are women—she, me, my grandmas—the connection from across the generation reaches for me—I embrace it. We are Finnish women; we feed our families—that is our love, that's part of how we do it.

The woodstove crackles cheerfully. Little helper-boy crawls over to dig in gramma's special drawer. :) I decide to stay home from church. Quick nap on the couch. Kids and Gregg go off. Baby Braxton and I are home getting the lunch ready. I gather greens and twigs to fill jars and vases. I make the table pretty—because we search for beauty. Put the finishing touches on the food. Baby and I play. Sweetness. Branches scrape against the window reminding me of the passing season; I look out and see the crystals, the blue sky.

The fire snaps, it is burning low. Opening the door, the squeak and clank immediately sweep me back to the farm. The sweet smell of burning alder and the hiss of the fire resonate. The memories squeeze; it's almost too much to take in.

I sit down hard on the chair by the farm table; dad is stoking the fire, just in from morning chores. "Good morning, Viv," he would say. "Hi dad." I'd like to say. The missing of him gathers in my throat. Wow, the influence a dad has on his sons and daughters. The living of a life and the brevity of it. . . The thought floats.

I turn back and kiss the grandson, admiring his fat little hands and twiggy hair. He giggles and sticks out his tongue; I do the same. The whole family arrives for lunch. The littles bounce in, grinning, and showing off their hats. Where did these small sweethearts come from—how did we get so lucky?

We pray and feast. My heart tugs; there's one missing from around the table. Tall and blonde. Visiting other places. The beautiful daughters want to take pictures. They pose and clown. How did this happen? All my girls grown or almost grown. Beautiful, poised, and successful. I'm the mom, admiring them from behind the camera.

What is a life, the meaning of it, I ponder. They laugh at each other, at the day. They touch and hug and make silly faces. I am a part, but not. They are sisters. I understand.

Time for the travelers to leave. Hugs and then the out-of-towners go, just as quickly as they came. . . Resting and playing with the other little grands. Funny little kids. Grampa drops off our teenagers at friends' houses, then takes a rest, some of us pack up and go to the park.

Sister falls asleep, mama is tired. Little boy, daddy, and gramma go to play at the jungle gym. He climbs on the play structure like a spider. His little crack shows over the top of his pants. His warm woolen sweater cuddles his tummy. Cute blue hat covers his ears; he shivers, wants to come down. "Too high," he whispers.

Daddy puts him in the swing, pushes him up against the blue sky. He laughs, a little scared. "Do it again, daddy," he giggles. Gramma goes for a little walk. "Come back soon, gramma" he orders.

I walk and then find them by the river. Sitting on a rock, he's fishing. His little curved stick touching the clear stream. Reflections of trees stand gracefully on the water. The perfection astounds. Time to go. We hold hands. His cold and small. Fits into mine just right. "You and grandpa come to my house," he declares. We discuss. "Bye-bye sweetheart, talk to you later. Tell sister gramma says bye."

Small brain and deep blue eyes consider. Sweetness and imp blend. "I won't," he decides. Daddy and I laugh, despite ourselves. Good-bye you sweet little gremlin. I walk on.

The moments. Our lives. Touching and blending, connected. Smiles, hugs, activities, small hands, good food, conversations.

Then all is quiet—it is over.

Back home. Grandpa had moved some furniture back into place. Gramma vacuums and cleans. I take two leaves out of the table. Expand and contract. Ebb and flow. Full house, then empty. Heart full, eyes leak. I ask God to hold my heart, my overwhelming emotions.

The connecting of the generations. I once was just a daughter, now a mom, the gramma. Wow. . . How? How did this happen so fast? . . . Traditions. The family members. The ones missing for now. The ones gone on to eternity, the ones to come.

And such it goes. Holding hands, touching hearts. Making meaning and clasping the moments, holding them close. And so it goes . . . And I attempt to write my thousand words for the pictures in my heart.

Farming

Today I made some mashed potatoes with hamburger and vegetable gravy. Yum! Comfort food at its finest! —something my mom used to make while we were growing up. Reminded me of those years working on the home farm.

Yesterday I drove around the gentle rolling hills of farm country here in the UP. It was a brilliant lovely fall day. I didn't see too many working farms, just a few. But lots of relics, remnants of early humble human existence— cause for contemplation.

I ran into a sign for the Hanka Homestead. It was a preserved farm from the late 1800s.

The country path meandered a long way out. The sun sparkled through the brilliant leaves as my tires crunched down the dirt road. I rolled the windows down all the way so I could take it all in.

It was so fresh and glorious. The farm was closed for the season. This farm girl could only look at it longingly over the fence. The Finnish flag flip-flapped in the breeze. The preserved wooden structures sat soundly on their foundations.

I read the placards and documentation about the farm. It was as I suspected. These Finnish people, our ancestors, were hard-working folks. The Scandinavian people were pretty much the low men on the totem pole when they arrived here. They often did many jobs just to make a living. In fact, the farms they were able to purchase were called stump farms—you can guess why. Every tree and stump had to be removed by hand, with maybe the help of a horse or two.

But this Hanka farm was set up pretty neat. The house was built first and the barn built next. The rest of the buildings followed. The smoke sauna was used for birthing, social interaction, cleansing, curing ailments, smoking fish and meat, and preparing the dead for burial. It was a well-used facility.

Cows were milked twice a day in the milk house, and the milk was stored in metal milk cans in the cool stream under the small milkhouse building.

There was the blacksmith shop, and the root cellar, the granary, the chicken coop, the woodshed and a machine shed.

A sign at the farm reads that most Finnish immigrants came to America to escape working for the Russian czar on large industrial farms. They wanted life on their own terms. These terms included a lot of back-breaking work, self-reliance and good ol' Finnish sisu.

These early Finnish farmers, not only worked the land in the summer, but in the other months, they trapped animals and sold the furs, fished for commerce and individual use, and logged when possible. These ancestors represent the dreams, work ethic and diligent character of thousands of Finnish immigrants.

They came together to make hay, log, and sometimes even to play baseball on Askel Hill. The women got together for a cup of coffee or a chat here and there. They occasionally traveled a short distance to visit family or friends.

As I read their history and breathed in the fresh country air, I walked where they toiled so many years ago. I paused to reflect on what life must have been like. I wondered if they enjoyed hamburger gravy over mashed potatoes. Or was it smoked fish and root vegetables?

I can only imagine. It's hard to put my modern-day mind back to such simple rugged conditions. We have it so easy on many fronts. But maybe their minds were clearer. Can you imagine not having the babel of the internet in your head? Or not needing to exercise, because your life was full of physical exertion? Or not having to sort and weed through your stuff, because you only have essentials? "Running to town" and all the stress that entails just wasn't an option.

As changes came through the years, sometimes they were met with applause, sometimes they were resisted, and sometimes we can only see in retrospect what was the true cost or blessings to families and society.

In any event, I'm glad they took time for community and friendship—definitely essentials for making it through life under any conditions.

Fall Family Blessings

I love spending time with my family doing the simple things, don't you? The simple things that usually do not make it into the photo albums, but the things that make it into the pages of life. Things like getting together and chopping apples, making applesauce, smelling "fall." Watching a small boy carve sticks and dream of knights in battles. Taking turns on the apple-corer-peeler-slicer, watching as the peels curl gently into a bowl and on the floor. Sticky floor, messy sink, lots of dirty pots and bowls.

Daughters that express love to each other and the beautiful smiling, squishy nieces and nephews. Putting them down long enough to make yummy desserts and wash a few dishes. Another daughter entertaining the grandson with sticky bubbles and huge balloons. Squeals, shouts, and the bangs of popped balloons. The young mom of the house organizing it all effortlessly. Dad of the home taking over with his sweet little daughter when he comes home from work (not that she needs holding, but who can resist?) Finishing with the working girl coming for supper with the rest of the men.

Garden-fresh lettuce, lots of pretty chopped veggies, taco chicken.

Giving thanks for all these blessings.

The pictures didn't make it into the album, but they are tucked into the special places in our hearts.

Shekinah Glory and God's Favor

Today I'm thinking about God's favor. As His children, it rests on us. His favor, His grace. Isn't that a nice thought? He looks on us with love and compassion. He thinks good thoughts toward us continually. He sings over us with love. He will never leave us or forsake us. And He answers our prayers—every time. That's favor! That's wonderful, life-giving, joy-building favor. It makes me smile, glad to be alive.

Yes, today I'm thinking about this favor I have, that surrounds like this all-too-familiar Pacific Northwest fog. Favor that seeps into our bones, transforms our thinking, puts joy in our hearts. This seeping favor. A year or so ago, I had a very sweet teacher at Clark College. She just smiled as she taught us about our ecological footprint and other Environmental Science-y things.

One day I was riding with her to go observe the layers of the earth at a park. We were talking about life and she said, "Well, Vivian, that's because you have favor." Others were in the car; she was speaking in code. God's code; I had favor. I hadn't heard it expressed that way before. Up to that point, the teacher and I had never discussed our faith, but she knew I had favor and I sensed Shekinah Glory about her. Isn't that beautiful? . . .

I was looking for the doo-hickey that plugs into my computer to make my mouse work. I wondered where in the world it could be. I asked my husband if he had taken it; he said no. But he leaned over to look at a large envelope with a Velcro-clasp that was lying on the table. "What's that?" he said. It was my doo-hickey, stuck to the Velcro. That's favor. Thank you, Jesus. So, may you be blessed today as you revel in God's favor. All these little blessings, all day long. He always answers, right on time.

May you make peace with the fog of this life and snuggle into your Shekinah Glory as you bless the world.

Not Codependent, but Dependent on God

This day I will concentrate on the inner meaning of the Commandment "Thou shalt love thy neighbor as thyself." I will accept myself, for that is the primary condition under which the good in me can grow. Unless I am at peace with the child of God I am, I cannot love and help my neighbor. Regrets are vain. They intervene with the good I could do today, the making of the better person I want to be tomorrow.

Live and let live. Having felt so overly responsible for other people's choices and actions, it can be a great struggle to grant others the dignity to make decisions for themselves and allow them to deal with the results. We use this slogan as a reminder to get off their backs and "let" them live.

Let go and let God. This slogan gives us permission to replace stress, worry, and suffering with serenity and faith. It's okay to relax and let life happen. We can rest assured that the answers, choices, actions, and thoughts we need will come to us when the time is right because we have placed them in the hands of God.

I try to give priority to taking care of myself. I eat good nutritious food at sensible hours. I make a serious effort to exercise every day, either walking or playing with my children or grandkids. I read my devotion every morning. I make every effort to think positive, affirming thoughts, and seek God or call a friend when I am unable to do so on my own. I also make a daily gratitude list, a mental list of everything wonderful in my life, from the sunrise to a project that is going well or a funny joke told by a friend. It is amazing how much I have to be grateful for, when I look for it. Mmmm. Good truths. Be blessed. (adapted from Codependent No More – ideas from Al Anon)

Conflict Resolution

Pray – even during communication

Listen to understand

Breathe – slow down

Self-control!

Note positive changes in myself and others

Use shared and creative parenting (or other group) – collaboration

Synergy – together we can accomplish more

No stories of what I think something is; wait, and listen

No criticizing

Build others up – no attacks

Withhold judgmental, evaluative, blaming language

Become softer and open up for transformation

Embrace both/and philosophy – we all can be both heroes and villains

Approach the table with a confident and positive attitude

Ask questions, listen to learn

Give and receive grace and forgiveness

My Paternal Grandmother's Strong Courage

I'm working on a short book about my grandma Helen Ranta Mattila. In the process I discovered my great grandma, Hilma Laminen Mattila... What a courageous woman! Lots of sisu, right there!!

Hilma Laminen was born in 1869 and lived in the Ruovesi area of Finland. While she was in school, she lived in the house of composer Jean Sibelius. "He is widely regarded as his country's greatest composer, and his music is often credited with having helped Finland develop a national identity during its struggle for independence from Russia." (found online)

Her sister Ida had moved to New York City. Hilma was waiting to go there also; Ida, or another friend was supposed to send her a ticket. She kept waiting.

Meantime, she married Emil Mattila in Finland. Shortly after marriage, her ticket to America arrived! Imagine her excitement! Determined as ever, she packed her bags and boarded the ship to America. . . America!

She went to work to earn money for Emil to join her, and also so they could buy a house.

She worked hard and saved money, then went back to Finland. Her daughter Elvi was born in Finland and then they all came to America. Finally, she felt like she was home!

They knew other Finns in Ironwood, so they settled there. They joined forces and bought the house at 433 East Tamarack Street. Five more children joined the family. Back in the day, they used to say that God provided a bread basket with every child. There was always enough. Emil worked in the iron mines and died of stomach cancer in 1927.

Hilma didn't speak much English, so she had a hard time communicating with those of her grandchildren who didn't speak Finn. She lived until 1963. She lived 94 years on this earth, striving to build a better life in America for her family and for herself. Well done, great grandma! Well done. She had a testimony of faith; I am looking forward to meeting her one bright day!

Wrinkled Pants and Active Noodles

I shuffled into the darkened living room one morning to find my youngest crouched on the floor, in his boxers, huddled over his jeans that were carefully laid out with a heavy book holding down the bottom part of the leg of his pants. They were more than slightly wrinkled because he put them in the wash wadded up and inside out. And no, I'm not an immaculate washer - I figure I'm not going to work harder on their stuff than they're willing to work on it; he knows clothes should go in the dirty clothes basket ready to go in the washing machine.

"What are you doing?" I asked him.

"I'm straightening my pants" he responded.

I figured he had made a good stab at trying to deal with the consequence of his choice. "Do you want me to iron them?" I queried.

"Would you?!" He exclaimed.

"Sure, I can do that," I told my smiling boy.

"Thanks, mom!" :):) . . .

I just wonder how long he thought it would take the fat book to straighten his horribly wrinkled jeans?

But, I applaud him for using his noodle and making an effort.

Expressing Anger Appropriately

The following are guidelines for responsible expression of anger.

1. Verbally state the anger. Say, "I am angry."

2. Distinguish between venting and acknowledging anger.

3. Agree that you will never attack each other in a state of anger.

4. Work to find the stimulus for the anger. It will not go away just because it is expressed. What is causing it?

In addition, we know that constructive conflict is never abusive or violent. Breaking down conflict into manageable pieces is a constructive way to fractionation (reducing the intensity of emotion in conflict). When I choose to downsize a conflict, I also am choosing to downsize emotion.

Because change is difficult, I have to choose to alter my emotionally-based behavior. When we care about our relationships, we feel a strong impetus to work toward these difficult changes. Radical self-responsibility means we take seriously our own possibilities for infusing hope and positive change into the world.

People cannot be identified as villains, heroes, good and bad people, or healthy and unhealthy members. Because everyone affects everyone else, looking for chain reactions, rather than pinpointing one person as the culprit is a way to move toward healthy resolution. Moving from blaming to acknowledging how my behavior affects the others is the first step to more constructive conflict. It is so invigorating to realize that the conflict cycle can be changed by any one person changing his or her behavior. (Matthew 18:15-17; Ephesians 4:31-32; Proverbs 15:1; Matthew 18:15; Ephesians 4:26; James 4:1-6; Colossians 3:13)

Your King Desires your Beauty

As I was walking by the river I was talking with the King. He reminded me about you—all of you princesses who sometimes feel like withered, crippled warriors—fighting on and on and on in the dry, cracked desert. "Look up, daughter," He seems to say. He wants to draw you close to the living stream, where your feet will be firmly planted and watered, where the heavenly rains will refresh your parched heart.

He is breathing His breath—His very spirit into your parched heart. He is lovingly gazing at you, offering Himself for you. Drink Him in, taste and see that He is good. Rest in His love, feel His peace, dance in His arms. You are His princess, His heart's desire. He will give you the strength, the courage, the grace to continue on.

Blessings, warrior princess, your King greatly desires your beauty—beautifully broken as we all are.

(Isaiah 41:10; John 3: 16; 1 John 4:16; Eph. 3:17-19; Psalm 118:6; Psalm 147:3; 1 John 4:10)

Suggestions on How to Live a Happy & Rewarding Life:

Take time to smell the roses.
Take a nap on Sunday afternoon.
Drink eight glasses of water a day.
Never deprive someone of hope; it might be all they have.
Be thankful for every meal.

Don't be afraid to say, "I'm sorry."
Don't take good health for granted.
Don't interrupt.
Don't tailgate.
Improve your performance by improving your attitude.
Listen to your children.

Leave everything a little better than you found it.
Keep it simple.
Keep good company.
Keep your promise.
Be kinder than necessary.
Take good care of those you love.

How to Talk so Kids will Listen and Listen so Kids Will Talk

I read a terrific book for one of my classes called, "How to talk so kids will listen and listen so kids will talk." Wow! So much good info. Wish I had known this stuff years ago. It's awkward at first to learn to do things differently, but it is so worth it!

So far, the book is saying how important it is to empathize with our kids' feelings instead of trying to fix things and provide answers. Sounds like if we take care of this early enough, we will not get into the codependent and control issues in later years. However, if you are in the later years, "Losing control and liking it" for dealing with teens and "Codependent no more" for dealing with self and the rest of the world are great books. It's so freeing to know we don't have to have all the answers.

So, when one of my children gets angry and frustrated because he/she can't find something, instead of telling her/him to learn to put things away and jump in and help find the missing object, I now can say, "wow, you're really frustrated." Then the conversation progresses in more expressions from the child, more acknowledgment of feelings by me. Child calms down and finds what is missing. Who knew? No lectures, no judgment, no condemnation.

The book has story after story of parents letting their kids express their feelings with words or pictures, without judgment. Then, saying things like "you are really angry." And letting them keep drawing and maybe talking. The kids calm down. We don't need to jump in and tell them how to feel, that their feelings are wrong, or how to fix their problems. They figure it out on their own.

If, they need help, or if we need to seek help, (lots of times it's the parents who have control/anger issues!) we do so. Rationally and calmly. Or, when in a store and the kid wants everything, instead of the usual battle taking place, fantasize with them. "Let's write it down!" Especially for younger kids the validation of putting their wants onto a list helps them calm down. One little boy told his sister, "Tell mom what you want, she'll put it on the list!" Isn't that precious!

Life has its sweetness. . . Lord, show us your ways, give us your wisdom. And lead us to the help we need so we can be strong, so we can help our kids be healthy, and so our families can thrive. Thank you, LORD.

A Boy Remembers Grandpa

I was four when my grandpa died. I did not think that it was a big deal because I was only four. My family and I went to see grandpa in his coffin at the church. We waited in line until it was our turn to see grandpa. I got scared because he was just lying there not breathing, not moving. He looked like a mannequin.

After the service, we went to bury him. Dad drove to the cemetery where grandpa was being buried. I got out of the car and saw my friends. I wanted to go play but my mom said, "No, come here." When I looked down, the pit where grandpa was going to be buried was a six-foot drop; I ran to my mom.

It took a few hours and then we drove home. Everyone was sad.

I will always miss my grandpa.

It is Well with my Soul

Sometimes I get discouraged about all that is wrong in the world—the abuse, addictions, brokenness, pain, neglect, etc. etc. Living in a neighborhood, a person hears all kinds of things. (Sometimes I wonder if people hear questionable things coming from our house.) Sometimes I have heard people yelling loudly. I have heard a father tell his little girl he did not love her. She started bawling her head off. Then the dad said, "Aww, I was just kidding." How sad is that?

I have heard chickens crowing at awful hours and a kid screaming hysterically. (After investigating with binoculars from the upstairs window, I found out he was only getting a hair cut!

But sometimes, a person gets a blast of sweetness and pure joy.

A few days ago, my daughter went outside on our deck and heard a little girl singing "It is well with my soul" at the top of her lungs. . . Is that precious or what?! Can you picture her? Arms swinging wide, head tipped back, and singing out of the fullness of her heart.

Thank you, Jesus, for the reminder from a child. . . Lord, help us to open our windows and sing of your goodness. . . It is well with my soul!

The Wonder of Small Boys

So, the other day we were driving by a cow pasture almost in Vancouver, and my son says, "Mom, there's a cow!" I suppose he was surprised to see a cow that close by town. Then he corrected himself and gave me the giggles by stating, "Actually it's not really a cow, but more like a teen-ager cow, you know, a smaller one."

******

I feel the weight of his scrutinizing stare as I'm following the text in church. He leans over and whispers, "Mom, do you have a double chin?" I stifled my impending outburst and whispered back, "what do YOU think?" He nods and continues, "I was just wondering because Billy (our grandson) has like five." . . . Well, at least I'm in good company. And I guess some of our most important questions are answered in church. :)

******

He tells his dad-turned-barber, "take it easy on my head, it's full of bumps."

******

We're sitting in church, the message touches me, I start to cry. My son notices and leans forward for a better look. "Mom, are you crying?" He whispers loudly. "Yes," I sniffle/giggle. "Why?" He reasonably questions. "Because I'm overwhelmed by God's love" I simply state and begin mopping my eyes and nose. As I'm distracted in the folds of the tissue, I feel a small skinny arm slide around my shoulders. He nestles in; I smile and thank God for small boys with skinny arms and big hearts.

Hey Vivy, How's my Girl?

"Hey Vivy! How's my girl?" I heard the familiar voice and whirled my cart around to give a long-time friend a hug, in the salad dressing aisle. . .

Growing up, there was a family that was special to our family. Many of my siblings and I worked for them through the years. I did yard work, house cleaning, house sitting, and babysitting for them. These people were kind to me. They thought I was talented and special.

The mother took me shopping once and bought me new clothes for school. She made me sandwiches on white bread and gave me Coke. (Growing up with homemade brown bread and an occasional soda, this seemed like super special treatment!) She drove a big black car that looked like a limo as she drove up our muddy driveway to pick me up. They treated me special.

The daughter thought I was the best babysitter in the world. The mother has now passed on but every once in a while, I bump into the daughter in the store. And that's when she says to me, "Hey Vivy! How's my girl?" That phrase brings back all those good feelings of being loved and cherished, of new clothes and Coke, of feeling special.

It reminds me that we all need people to believe in us, to breathe life and hope into our lives. To make us sandwiches on white bread.

It also reminds me that someday, I will see someone from true royalty. The someone who delivered me from the miry pit, who came for me in His chariot. And He is going to say, "Hey Princess! How's my girl?"

Worship "with" my Mother-in-law

Worship. That's what's on my mind.

I'm here at my mother-in-law's house in Michigan. Yesterday I went to the church she has attended for years and years. Her husband died 3 months after our wedding; she was a widow for many years. Her daughter lives in the same town and they were best friends for all that time. I'm thankful for my faithful mother-in-law and her daughter.

I felt the peace of God there in her church, with her people. I felt thankful that this place and these people have been her place of belonging for these 34 years that she's been a widow. I thought of all the Sundays that she went to church and then did other Sunday things. She's not feeling well now, so she didn't come with me.

I enjoyed the liturgy, the prayers. The main message I received was to draw others into fellowship with Jesus. So good! The song "Precious Lord, take my hand" brought tears to my eyes . . . There's so much goodness in fellowship.

I breathed it all in. God is faithful.

Battered and Broken,
God LIVES in the Praises of his People

God lives in the praises of His people. And if our God is for us, who can stand against?!

Awhile back, God took us from the inspiring heights of a mountaintop experience—viewing the glorious Crater Lake in Oregon—through the valley of shadows, a place where we were totally dependent on Him, and Him alone. He showed me how our prayers matter; how we are to bring our requests to Him with Thanksgiving. He showed me how He is always good, always working things for our good.

My prayers turned from, "Oh, God, please deliver us!" to, "Father, I know you have this worked out, please help us to trust you." And we praised Him in the storm and through the valley. As we started climbing the mountain to view the Crater, our vehicle began acting up, my husband knew it was the transmission.

We began praying for deliverance and drove slowly along. The majesty of God's creation took my breath away. Only a might God could have created all the beautiful vistas. The lake in the crater is a blue like you have never seen. Almost 2000 miles deep, only the azure rays reflect back. Trees and sharp banks rim the lake; a cone is formed in the center. The awesomeness of it all and my smallness humbled me to tears. And to think that the God who created all that beauty, has more thoughts toward me than the hairs on my head. It's simply amazing.

Praying and singing, we made our way toward a town 100 miles away. God lives in the praises of His people, doesn't He? Well, amazingly we made it to town. But once we got there, the transmission completely gave up the ghost. Now, what to do? We tossed around ideas and made phone calls. We were about 3 hours from home.

A text came from a friend who was out of town . . . "what's ours is yours." How do you describe the humble gratefulness to that kind of offer? Tears in my eyes, a lump in my throat. Or, as I texted my friend, "I have lumps in my eyes and everyone's singing your praises!" She texted back, "All praise to God." That's our God. That's his people. And our hearts are full.

As much as the mountaintop experiences inspire us, it truly is in the valley where growth takes place. We need both. Our son said he prayed most of the 100 miles to town. Our daughter said she knew God would work things out. As we got ready for bed after our exhausting day, my husband prayed a humble prayer of thankfulness and blessing to our wonderful Abba. Thank you, God, that you live in the praises of your people. Help us to give thanks in ALL things.

Paths Ordained

I have been thinking about the blessing of being involved with diverse people in various groups. In these groups, I have received and I have given.

My mom used to tell us, "If you're feeling down, do something for someone else." That's good advice. Not the brain's first response to depression, but even "expert" studies now show that doing acts of service is the best way to get out of a funk. The happy endorphins that are released in the brain as we do good deeds are exactly what our brain and body need. How marvelous is that? Positive thoughts and thankfulness change the chemicals in the brain!

I have been involved with a few different groups and individuals. For me, these groups are for a season and then I move on. I picture this as a wide beautiful path. I'm walking through tall, shade-giving trees, with a beautiful vista opening up in the distance. The sun is shining and walking beside me and talking along the way is Jesus.

You may have a different "picture" of life, but that's mine. So, as I walk, other paths open, people join us and we join others and the path of life just keeps meandering along—but along the way, we give and receive. Grace, mercy, and love.

Today I was thinking back to all the marvelous people I've met and have been close with even in the past few years; I marvel how well God has taken care of me as I do His will with JOY, doing my part in the tasks He brings to me. I am not saying I always do my best or accomplish these things without stubbing my toes and tripping a time or two, but I am learning as I go too.

My prayer for each of us is that we can be blessed and be a blessing to others as we walk in the path in which our Creator invites us to walk. (1 Peter 2:21; Isaiah 41:10; 1 John 2:3-6; Matt. 11:28-30; Eph. 4:15; John 13:34-35)

Jesus Became a Servant

Today I am reflecting on and thankful that Jesus not only understands our sorrow and grief, but He became a servant. That he set the example of washing the blood, poop, dirt, etc. off the disciple's feet—a job left for the lowliest servant. That's our Jesus.

He cares for us tenderly, washes us carefully, dies on the cross for us and forgives us fully. That's our Jesus. He's the example.

Today I'm thankful that I know Him in the power of the resurrection. I'm thankful for his example of service. He never says, "I've done my time. Now it's your turn."

Sometimes I get weary. But then, I remember Jesus.

In His last days, he wasn't deciding what trinket he could buy for Himself, or how He could show off His status or power, He was washing feet—serving others.

Jesus, I am humbled by the messages I hear in your word and by your servants. Thank you for becoming a servant. Thank you for setting the example. (1 Peter 4:10-11; Acts 20:35; Galatians 5:13-14; John 13:12-14; Mark 9:35; Mark 10:44-45)

To all you Gals out there!

1.**You are Valuable**: You are so important and so valued that I will protect you with rules and boundaries because I love you. Someday you will understand that there is safety and comfort within those restrictions.

2.**Your Worth Isn't Based on Your Appearance**: You are beautiful–not because you might be wearing a new outfit or have a fresh hair-do–your worth is not found in your appearance, the opinions of others, or yourself. You are beautiful because you were created in the image of God. Your appearance has little to do with true beauty and your worth is not wrapped up in looking good or being perfect.

3.**You Don't Need a Guy:** A boy doesn't complete you, God does. Chasing or enticing or wanting a guy doesn't make you attractive and it doesn't make you a woman. Trust God's timing for if or when God brings you a husband.

4.**You Are Amazing**: I am proud of you. You are enough. Out of all the girls in the world, I would always choose you. You might be tempted to spend a lot of time in life trying to prove your value to others. I want you to know you are loved, just like you are. Today and forever.

5.You Don't Have to Believe What You Hear: Because there will be mean girls in your life, peers with pressure and adults in your world who will let you down and have low expectations of you. Listen to the voice of Jesus, who has a good plan for your life and who loves you best.

6.You Have Me (or someone like me): No matter what happens in life, the ups and downs that will come your way, the losses and gains, I will be there for you. You can talk to me about anything. Anytime. More importantly, you always have Jesus.

7.You Can Change the World: You can dream big and can accomplish whatever you wish. You can do so with God by your side and you do not need a boy or society to make it happen. I am standing with you and by you, watching you fly.
Adapted from: http://wearethatfamily.com/2013/03/raising-daughters-in-a-world-that-devalues-them-7-things-we-must-tell-them/

Perspective

Perspective is everything.

Wondering what to serve company for supper seems like small potatoes when compared to having no potatoes.

Having an ache in my foot is bearable when I think of those who have spent time in wheelchairs, doubled over in pain.

Experiencing the theft of treasured possessions cannot compare to the theft of sexual innocence suffered by so many through familial abuse.

Dying peacefully, surrounded by loved ones, cannot compare to feeling so desperate that you take your own life.

Feeling hopelessly lost, burdened, and unloved is the abyss where Satan wants people to be; but our wonderful Creator has made a way, through His Son for all to share in vibrant, loving, joyful community—there is no comparison!

Father God, please help us all to respond to these real issues, to meet the hurting in this world, at your perfect point of intersection. Father, only you can equip us, only you can stop the pain. We ask that you move mercifully in each of these real situations.

We trust you, Abba. We are willing to do your bidding. Give us your perspective, Abba. Thank you; we praise you.

(Psalm 69:30; Psalm 100:4; Ephesians 5:3-4; 2 Samuel 22:47; 1 Cor. 15:57; *Col.* 2:6-7; 1 Thess. 5:16-18)

Suffer with the Suffering

This is an incredible story. During the Nazi invasion of Europe, many people devoted their lives to non-violently helping the Jews escape the brutality of the Nazi regime. Recently I watched a documentary called "Prince of Peace, God of War," which addresses the issues of war, peace and the Christian involvement in those activities. One of the doctors discussing these issue in the documentary, named Tony Compolo, told an incredible story that answered my question of "How then does a Christian respond to brutality and evil?" This is his story:

The SS troops had come to a town in Bulgaria to round up Jews heading for Auschwitz and certain death. It was a damp misty night as the Jews huddled at the station in terror. As they waited, out of gloom and fog strode a seven-foot-four Christian priest named Metropolitan Curo, robes swirling, long beard hanging to his waist; he was followed by 300 congregants. This group reached the barbed wire enclosure and were told by the SS troops they could not go into the area where the Jews waited. The priest laughed at them, pushed the machine guns aside, and entered. The fear-drenched Jews looked to the Christian priest wondering what he would say.

This is how he responded, from the book of Ruth, "Whither thou goest, I will go. Your people will be my people. Your God will be my God." The tearful cheering from the Jews and the 300 others drew thousands from their homes. They surrounded the brutalized Jews. The SS troops knew no Jews would be getting into the waiting train cars; they pulled out of the station— defeated and empty. Furthermore, no Bulgarian Jew ever died in a concentration camp during the Nazi regime. . . The response as Dr. Compolo stated—the priest and townspeople identified with the suffering and suffered with them. This, he said, was the teaching of Christ.

(Gal. 6:2; 1 Peter 5:10; John 16:33; Rev. 21:4 -Mark 13:13; Matthew 10:17; Acts 14:22; Rev. 2:10)

Perfection – in Christ

"Mom, Joy has a sixth finger," one of my kids announced as I joined them to admire our new granddaughter. I stopped in disbelief, not sure what to say. So I looked. Sure enough, dangling by a mere strip of skin, was a tiny digit. I guess it is hereditary on her daddy's side. I never knew such things happened. It seemed amazing that an extra little finger (complete with a nail) could form. It is astonishing that all the DNA and nutrients could get down to that finger through that slight bit of skin by which it was attached! It's formation itself is a miracle! It will be removed one way or another, just like it was with her ancestors. Just a teeny blip and on to . . . perfection.

But, isn't she already perfect? Of course, her tiny dangling finger will be removed; it would be cruel not to do so. But what about all the other imperfections (as we call them) that cannot be changed? Why does God allow these things to happen? The biblical example is so that He will be glorified. Glorified. Lifted up and given praise.

I praise you Jesus for the gift of Joy! For her little dangling digit that feels soft in my fingers. I praise you that it can be easily removed. I praise you that you allow all things for our good. Thank you for the reminder that our life is but a vapor. That we all are connected to you through sinew and blood. That we may feel like we are dangling by the slightest string, but that we are actually held firmly in your grasp—double clasped, and you will never let go! That you are able to sustain us through that which is not visible.

Thank you, Jesus, that you have all things securely under control. That NOTHING goes unnoticed. That nothing is without reason. That you will be glorified! Praise you Jesus! Praise you for the gift of abundant life in you.

Praise you for sweet Joy. (Is it possible that I love her more, with her little dangling finger that felt so strange at first?) Oh Jesus! I am humbled! Thank you for the reminders.

These People are Just SO Different Than Me!!

Some days I'm juiced! Pumped. Ready to pop out of my skin. Why? Because sometimes, I'm standing on the cusp of a new adventure, ready to take one big Tigger leap into the abyss!

Woowee! I can't see the end of the leap, but my springs are loaded and I am prepared for take-off! Have you been there? Can you relate? If so, you are a Merchant/Innovator like me. (from the Core Value Index survey)

You know the feelings. It's when you're brimming with new ideas, exciting propositions, adventures waiting to happen. And it's not a blind leap; you've checked it out and it falls right into what you are wired for. You're connecting with new people, ideas are going wild, excitement is in the air! Fireworks are going off.

However, if you are not like me, you may be thinking, "That's one wild woman who's completely off her rocker! She's so far gone-zo, she's off the porch!" And I would reply, "You're completely right and it feels WONDERFUL!"

But if you're with the "she's-off-the-porch-and-it's-not-a-good-thing" crowd, you are a Builder/Banker (CVI survey). You like structure, plans, completion; you want to know the end of the story. You sometimes wonder if half the world has gone crazy. You and Paul Harvey would sit on the porch analyzing the situation til the cows come home. And you know what? The pokey, structured things you normally do, frustrate us Merchant/Innovators to no end!

You're stodgy, stuck in the mud, fuddy-duddies (yes, I admit, that's just one way to look at it!). And here's the kicker. God (bless you, Father!) made us all. Somehow, he wants us all to live together, in community, at least somewhat peacefully. Are you smiling yet?

Weeelllll, the Maker wired us. So, friends, we need to learn about each other. Enjoy our differences. Go with the flow.

Embrace what God has set up. See each other as perfect imperfections, made in His image.

Boing! I'm outta here. See you on the other side!!!! Woowee!

I pray that we all can just stop, rest, and listen to the leading of the Holy Spirit. When God says "rest," we rest. When He says "pray," we pray. And when He says "move," we Move! Electrified by the joy of the Lord, which is our strength! No heavy burdens because we are yoked with Him and His burden is easy and His yoke is light. (Matt. 11:30; Col. 3:3; Acts 17:28; Gal. 6:9; 1 Cor. 3:16)

Decide that Family Matters

"God, we can't, you can, please help" . . . *Decide That Family Matters* . . . it is a very important to establish these ideas in family life. Teachings from Ephesians 4:17-32 set the groundwork. Additionally, choosing to love our family members in non-controlling, encouraging ways, adds value to our lives. Hallelujah! My spirit sighs with contentment; thank you, God.

Here are seven ways to demonstrate that your family matters: But, first read verses 17-24 about putting off the old man and putting on Christ; being made new in the attitude of our minds, putting on the new self, created to be like God in true righteousness and holiness. God understands what we are dealing with and He wants to help. . .

1) Talk truth – we want to live truthfully, in community, and in loving relationships that say "You matter." v. 25

2) Be angry appropriately – not in verbal abuse, in violence, or in wrath - v. 26

3) Share selflessly – do not be a physical or emotional drain – v. 28

4) Build benefit – build others up according to their needs, love in a way that matters to them, love in a way others can receive – v. 29

5) Give attention to God – do not grieve the Holy Spirit with sin; we are sealed for the day of redemption, walk in Christ – v. 30

6) Ban the big guns – get rid of bitterness, rage, anger . . . do not be hurtful, violent or abusive, if so - talk to someone, get help – v. 31

7) Forgive freely – be kind, a compassion listener, reconnect, rebuild, and forgive – v. 32

Faith not Sight

Sometimes I wander away (even for a short time) from God's truth and begin to focus on my (and other people's) failings and negative feelings. And I'm wondering if you do the same? Then we wonder where God is and why he isn't answering our prayers, why we are downcast and discouraged.

We have learned that God's love and presence are with us by day and His song is our sustenance at night, but sometimes we think we are called to walk by sight and not by faith! Completely opposite of our calling. Does this ever happen to you? . . .

Lord, when we start to focus on our circumstances and failures—our own and those of others, help us to remember you are FAITHFUL and TRUE, our Rock and Fortress! Help us to remember that our "hope is in you, our God!"

We will praise you! We must counsel ourselves (our forgetful selves) and not let our forgetful selves counsel us (by meditating on failures and circumstances-and stealing our praise and joy!). David, in the 42nd Psalm wonders why he is downcast. He is walking by sight and not by faith. His enemies are ever before him, taunting him. But then he remembers, as we must, that God is our hope, our love, our song. Praise you Jesus! Praise changes everything! . . .

Be blessed, dear friends, as you dive into the word today; He is our hope and our song! Bring your heart, full of your cares to him, pour it out. . . And return to praise. Meditate on his goodness and loveliness. His mercy, his grace. His compassion. His truth. His faithfulness. . .

Praise you Jesus! Thank you, LORD, that you are ever with us, our hope and our song.

(Psalm 40:3; Psalm 121; Psalm 42)

Faith or Fear

Today in the midst of the snowdrifts, I'm thinking about people, life, and our stories in the midst of the living of life. Our stories, what has happened in our lives, direct how we live our lives. But not only do our stories direct our lives, our responses and involvement in our stories indicate how we live the rest of our lives.

You see, as our stories unfold, how we connect to life is based in how we view life and the world. If we see our world as safe and warm, we react and interact with love or faith. Kindness, empathy, goodness, and mercy flows. If our world seems cold and scary, we live in fear. That's basically it. Two responses. We either live, act, and interact with love (faith) or fear.

When I started living with this knowledge, it changed everything (not that I get it right every time, but I'm on my way!). Each thought, each word, each action is a chance to show what I believe. Do I believe in a loving God, whose name is faithful and true, who will right all things and take care of me?

Or do I think I need to control all things and all people, do I not believe that God is faithful and true, sovereign and involved? Is my response to the world and the people in the world angry, controlling, bitter, or resentful?

Fear or faith, my friends. The choice makes all the difference.

(Mark 4: 35-41; Acts 17:11; Heb 11:6; Eph. 2:8-9; Prov. 3:5-6; James 2:14-26)

Be Angry and Sin Not

Feel your feelings. They are neither right or wrong, good or bad; they just are. Whew! What a relief.

What happens when we don't feel what we're feeling? We speed right by them into something more "acceptable" or familiar – like anger. Now there's a feeling we all know how to feel, right?! Sometimes our anger seems bigger than life. Huge! It takes on a life of its own, rampaging around and splashing on those around us. Ouch!

Psychologists used to say "Let it out! Express it!" What happened? Nothing was resolved and there were lots of really angry people walking around hurting others.

Now, even the secular psychologists say to deal with anger in healthier ways – deep breathing, journaling, meditating, waiting to cool down before dealing with whatever we allowed to push our buttons. Remember, we allowed the anger to control us; we did – no one else. The Bible says it best – "Be angry and sin not." Feel your feelings. Before the anger comes on like a hot steamroller – what came before it? Was it fear? Of what were you afraid? Was it pain? What is hurting you? Was it embarrassment? What is making you feel awkward? There are myriad reasons we get angry. Studies show continually expressing anger does all kinds of awful things to our bodies.

Isn't it better (harder initially) to just feel the pain or fear or whatever is causing the anger? Ouch. Just feel it and then we can deal with it. But behind the feeling are thoughts. Our thoughts control everything. Is our thinking faulty? Try saying your thoughts aloud, or journaling. Do your thoughts bear the light of day? Do they line up with the truth in God's word? What's really real? Or have we allowed our thoughts to become grossly out of proportion to reality? Back to the Word – "Think on what is true, honest, just, pure, lovely, commendable, praise-worthy." There are reasons God says what he does. His word helps us live our lives better – victoriously! In truth.

Stop the anger. Feel your feelings. Examine your thoughts and start "taking them captive to the obedience of Christ." The Bible says we have "the mind of Christ." Wow! Let's ask God to fill our minds with His thoughts. Selah!

Rockin with Poppa

I'm feeling blessed and super loved . . .

God is so good and takes care of all our needs, doesn't he? I'm having one of those "rocking in the chair with Poppa" moments. . .

We're sitting on the wide, North Carolina style front porch, wooden boards under our feet, there's a slight misty breeze. We're in the chair—me and Poppa. The wooden rocker is big enough for both of us (funny thing about being with Poppa, there's always just enough room).

We sit and rock gently; he pushes off with his sandaled feet— softly calmly. That's a good thing about Poppa, he takes things slow and gentle. His arms are around me, holding me, quietly, securely. His comforting robe surrounds. My head is on his shoulder, face turned toward His center; I breathe in his scent. Poppa.

A light wind blows; I smell salt in the air. Morning is coming; the sky is streaked with shades of pink and white. A sweet, peaceful sunrise. This is a time of refreshing, just me and my Poppa—on the porch.

"No worries" he seems to whisper in my ear. "Poppa's got you."

On our Way

Jesus came so that we might have abundant life, overflowing with God's mercy, justice, and love. This abundant life involves finding our vocation, our calling; it may be a life-long task. But once we find it and move in the direction of what is our true calling, we find peace, joy, and contentment.

Our vocation is where our deep gladness meets the world's deep need. I love that! Whatever it is that God instilled in our spirit that makes us uniquely us, the experiences that makes our heart sing and our spirit soar, that is our vocation, our calling! Through this discovery process, we run into snags and bumps and sometimes walls. However, once we are on our way, we engage in service to a world that desperately needs us.

In our places of brokenness and risky engagement with a hurting world, we find great communion with God. As we look for our vocation, we engage in some highly effective practices. We live attentively, listening to our higher calling, resisting powerful pressure and unexamined assumptions. We also live with others in a truthful, life-giving way.

We live in the real world; our lives are fleshly and imperfect; we are making imperfect progress. We live for the good of all; we address the reality of brokenness and sin in today's world. We are beacons of God's justice, mercy, and love.
Finally, we live in response to God. We find those who yearn for abundant life with God and others; we share our questions and lives with them. We are on our way to finding our vocation, by the grace of God.

The Abundant Life

I pray we are all living the abundant life that is ours in Christ! Jesus does not call believers "sinners." He calls us saints, a royal priesthood, the elect, blameless, righteous, faithful!

Yes, we know we sin, but that is not who we are, or what defines us! We live the resurrected life—in the power of the spirit - united with the Lord! We live in newness of life; old things are passed away! We are the light of the world - Jesus tells us to live as children of light! Not serving sin, looking to the failures of the past, or fearing the future. We live in the present, in the glorious power and strength of our LORD!

Romans 8:9-11 - "You, however, are controlled not by the sinful nature, but by the Spirit, if the Spirit of God lives in you. And if anyone does not have the Spirit of Christ, he does not belong to Christ. But if Christ is inside of you, your body is dead because of sin, yet your spirit is alive because of righteousness. And if the Spirit of Him who raised Jesus from the dead is living inside of you, he who raised Christ from the dead will also give life to your mortal bodies through His Spirit, who lives within you."

There is power in Jesus and in His wondrous name to heal anyone, to bring souls to a knowledge of salvation, to bring nations to knees in repentance (asking for forgiveness), and to transform our lives to be a beautiful reflection of Him!

Wow! Wow! Wow! Thank you, Jesus!

I'm Sorry

Scripture teaches us that saying, "I'm sorry," is part of the process of repentance, confession, forgiveness and reconciliation. By this process we stay in loving relationships with others and with God.

Because we are called to love sinners, we must continually forgive them. Love is saying, "I'm sorry," and it is saying, "I forgive you."

These two statements should be heard often in our homes. If they are rarely spoken, it indicates the practice of denial and hiding. If we do not apologize or express forgiveness, we are not being honest about our sin or the bitterness that is growing deep within our souls.

God, help up the be humble and say, "I'm sorry."

Gems from my Counseling Theory Professor

Life is not rocket science.
The Bible has all the answers.
Take time to reflect each day.
Make things right. Move on.
Be disciplined.
Do the task. Leave outcomes to God.
Set boundaries.
Keep learning; never stop.

Eat well.
Exercise daily.
Keep a clear mind.
Take plenty of time off.
Listen.
Cultivate good friendships; seek counseling if necessary.
Let go of dead weight and bad theology.
Laugh. Often.
Find truth.
Stay in the moment.
Forgive much.
Love always.
Receive and extend grace.
Model good behavior without expectations.
Be compassionate.
Look for God, do what He does.
Care for others.
Seek. You will find.

God Does Not Make Junk: Love Yourself Today!

1. **Recognize your special qualities**. . . Did God create you to be kind, artistic, honest, encouraging, funny? Post your list where you will see it every day

2. **Put your body back together** . . . All of it! No dissing your tush or tummy! Reconnect with your body by appreciating how God made it all work together to keep you going. Try yoga – the fluid movements are great for getting in touch with the wonders of the human body

3. **Remember the kid inside you**. Give yourself permission not to be perfect. Remember to nurture yourself and laugh a little (or a lot!)

4. **Enjoy your food**! Eating is pleasurable. So enjoy it! It gives us energy and sustains life. By giving ourselves permission to enjoy some of the foods we like, we will be less likely to overeat

5. **Indulge in body pleasures**. Get a massage, take a bath, use good smelly lotion or oils

6. **Speak positively**. To yourself. . . and others. If you catch yourself saying something negative, fight back with a compliment

7. **See the world realistically**. Don't compare yourself to people in magazines and movies. They are not real, and by comparing ourselves to them, we just feel bad about ourselves. The media and corporations want us to feel bad about ourselves so that we will spend lots of time, energy, and money continually working on our appearance. Fight back! Revel in who God made you to be--Reflecting His glory. Working in His kingdom! People come in different shapes and sizes and everyone is beautiful!

8. **Dress in clothes that fit**. Feel good now! Don't wait until you feel "perfect"

9. **Be active**. Movement and exercise can make you and your body feel terrific

10. **Thrive!** Living well will help you feel better about who you are and how you look. You are a unique, amazing person! God doesn't make junk!

11. **Renew your mind in God's truth** . . . you are the apple of his eye, his bride, his chosen vessel, created to do good works, his child, his treasure, his creation, his beloved, his redeemed, and worth singing about!

Adapted from a women's studies class . . . Women's Voices.

Hair Salon Trauma

As I was seated at the salon, the young stylist draped me with towels. He asked if I wanted my "usual" or the "special." Bravely I smiled, "I'll try the special."

When he brought out the used Windex bottle and started dousing my curls and the water began dripping down my back, I knew I may have gotten myself into a bit more than I bargained for. He chortled as I grimaced while the old black comb tugged its way through my resisting hair. "The best is yet to come!" He shrieked with delight. Then I heard what sounded like quarts of mousse being squirted all over my head. He deftly combed the white clouds of product into my locks and rubbed the excess clumps on the towel in my lap. My face contorted, I shut my eyes. I waited patiently for the next blast from the expert stylist.

All was quiet so I peeked one eye open. I had trouble focusing on the gap-toothed smile inches from my face; I'm not sure why he felt the need to peer into the crevices of my eyeball socket, but he did.

Disturbed, I asked him why he was inspecting me so closely. "All part of the job," he replied, "I wanted to see how you were liking it. By the way," he continued, "I will be charging you extra since I'm experimenting on you."

"What? Huh?" I croaked. The quarter he was charging for his service was hard to come by.

"In my world it works just the opposite," I protested.

"Well, you're in my chair and I can kick you out whenever I want" he reasoned. "By the way, mom, this is SO MUCH FUN!" He shouted gleefully. Then I saw him coming at me with the blow dryer in one small hand and the hairspray in the other. I shuddered and closed my eyes.

However, I had seen that gap-toothed grin again and thought, "Yeah, it's worth it; I'll pay his price."

Sociological Imagination

The Sociological Imagination is a quality of the mind that allows us to understand the relationship between our particular situation in life and what is happening at a social level. It is a way of looking at the world beyond our own immediate personal experience. It can take us into different worlds, very diverse from our own.

It helps us appreciate different viewpoints and understand how they may have come about. It also helps us the understand better how we developed our values, beliefs, and attitudes.

Sociological Imagination. The ability to understand "the intersection between biography and history," or the interplay of self and the world . . .

from "The Real World." Interesting. Btw – Do you know that 80% of what we know, we learn by teaching others? Thanks for listening.

Finnish Roots

History is very interesting to me... Especially when I can visit the actual sites where history was being made.

So, from what I can gather, in a book called, "Finns of Michigan's Upper Peninsula," and earlier reading a book by Carl Kulla, about the Laestadian movement, many of my Lapland ancestors came into this country through Hancock, Michigan, maybe after a short stop in New York.

They came after long journeys at sea, and they tried to assimilate into the culture. It seems some of them came with the intent of possibly returning to their original countries; they were hard-working people.

Many left improvised conditions, hoping for a better life in America. However, many of them were extremely poor in this new country also. Their homes let in the harsh environment, they slopped through muck in the streets, their clothes were scratchy and patched, their food had little variety, and they were prone to get bedbugs and lice. They were thankful if they had a sauna, or if they could use the public saunas.

The men worked as fishermen, farmers, loggers, and miners. The women maintained the homes and raised the children. If husbands died, women also had to go to work or take in laundry or boarders. The children attended the schools, and they learned the culture and then passed it on to their parents. In many cases, children also had to work to help support the family, sometimes children as young as five and six were needed to help care for younger siblings. It was a difficult time for all; survival was at the core of their existence.

Years passed, and some of our ancestors were able to gain a better foothold in this new land. Then they were able to afford items such as shoes for year-round, new coats and hats for the season, more pots and pans, furniture. They had time for vacations a few miles away. They found ways to celebrate life. They learned to laugh and have fun.

It's hard for us to who live in our affluent country to conceive of the harshness of their environment, especially with the cold

cold winters in upper Michigan, where many of them started; many died from illness, accidents or because of meager living conditions. The survivors were robust resilient people. I have their DNA.

Interestingly, most of us only know our ancestors back to maybe three or four generations. Those ancestors were the ones who came to America.

So the church-going people attended the state church in their countries of origin. Upon coming here, some of our ancestors were of the Laestadian Movement; (delivered from drunkenness and reindeer thievery, abandonment of families.)

I like to know where I come from and what made us the way we are. Stoicism and legalism were in our culture from the beginning. They had to learn how to live as Christ-followers, some of them had many superstitions that were involved in their earlier ways. They gave up finery because they thought that's what Christians did.

Many adults didn't read English. I'm not sure if they had many Finnish, Norwegian or Swedish Bibles. I know my dad had one, that was his father's. In many cases, it was from the children learning English at school, and then helping their parents learn English so they could read the King James Bible. In another historical book I read, it is apparent that the Holy Spirit was alive and active and working through all people—young and old. God is good.

My mother-in-law grew up in Toivola. Today there's one or two buildings standing in town. Back in the day there was at least a Church, a Cafe and a Store. She remembered going to them all.

She talked of a sweet childhood—working hard in the summer, staying cozy in the winter. Now she is gone, and most of the buildings have crumbled into dust.

Some of my relatives are buried in Eagle River and others in the Elo Cemetery by Otter Lake. They lived their lives making a living off the land, gathering with friends and worshipping God. They raised their families, learned American ways and thought of home. Their lives were a lot more difficult in some ways, but in other ways, they were a lot simpler. Stress came from working to make a living, but they didn't have the stress we have from our current culture, social media, corruption all around and a seemingly upside-down world.

Our shared history remains. These ancestors' struggles and victories are hard-wired into our DNA. They made us who we are, in all of our diverse ways.

My Reactions, My Relationship

My reactions to circumstances testify to the kind of relationship I have with Jesus and the effect He has on my heart. That is a sobering, centering thought.

In our everyday lives and communication, we know we do not want to be out of control; slaves to our circumstances, hormones, or other people's attitudes. We don't want to be:

1)exploders who shame ourselves,

2)exploders who blame others

3)stuffers who gather retaliation rocks for later use.

So, what to do, what to do? Well, we must remember feelings are indicators of what's going on inside, they are not dictators, we do not need to act on them. King Jehoshaphat (2 Chron. 20) provides a good guideline for retaining soul integrity in the heat of the moment.

1)Remember who you are. "The people came together to seek help from the Lord." We are Christ-followers, capable of making wise choices.

2)Redirect your focus to Jesus. "We do not know what to do, but our eyes are on you." Jesus, Jesus, Jesus. We know where our help comes from.

3)Recognize God's job isn't your job. Our job is obedient trust. "For the battle is not yours, but God's." (This also includes trying to control or fix others.)

4)Recite thanks and praises to God. "King J. appointed men to sing to the LORD and to praise him for the splendor of his holiness as they went out at the head of the army, saying: "Give thanks to the LORD, for his love endures forever." Wow! Our focus changes from what's wrong, to praising God for what's right. When my heart is full of praise, my emotions are not as easily prone to become unglued.

5) Realize reactions determine reach. "For God had given him (King J.) peace on every side." Wow! In the midst of it all, King J. honored God with his actions and reactions.

This was so good, I had to share it!
(From Unglued by Lysa Terkeurst)

Honor in Relationships: Keys to Success

Honor God, others, self

Decide how you'll serve others in genuine honor and love

Understand and believe you can do whatever you want in life with knowledge and skills. First you must gain the necessary knowledge in your chosen area of service and then practice applying that knowledge unto you become skilled

Who is going to be our master? We all serve someone or something. The choice is ours. Some choices lead to greater fulfillment, and others lead to enslavement or dissatisfaction. We can't blame anyone or anything else for our choices. Who will we serve? The psalmist says, "Bless the Lord, O my soul; and all that is within me, bless His holy name." The word blessing means to *bend the knee* before someone who is of highest worth. When we thought of blessing God, we imagined bending our whole life – our thoughts, feelings, body, and everything else that makes up who we are – before the Lord.

Honor simply means *deciding to place high value, worth and importance on another person by viewing him or her as a priceless gift and granting him or her a position in our lives worthy of great respect.*

A working definition would be:

 Treat others as special

Doing more than is expected

Having a good attitude

Anger, unjust criticism, unhealthy comparisons, favoritism, selfishness, envy, etc. are used against people we consider to be of little value. The lower value we attach to people, the easier we can justify dishonoring them with our words or treating them with disrespect.

See all people as part of God's family and treat them as priceless treasures. We honor God by recognizing that His worth is beyond any price; similarly, we honor others by considering people to be special gifts of God, that He has placed in our lives, for our good.

Viewing our family as an extension of God's family provides a leveling effect. We're all sinners needing equal grace, and each member is surrendering to the same Lord. Every day we fail and must confess our sin to the Father. Rather than looking for power over one another, we must learn mutual humility, acceptance, admonition, and love. Viewing the family as a subset of God's family helps people feel a part of a team, with honor providing a tight bond.

Bazaars and Christmas for Children in India

During my time in Upper Michigan, I was doing a few bazaars, making money for Christmas for the children we help support in India.

Yes, it probably would be easier and simpler just to send the money over. But I feel compelled to do things and spread the word, to involve other people to help pray for these beautiful children and their futures.

So I thrift, and package, and order pictures and make cards, and buy flour and yeast and cardamom, and more flour and yeast and eggs and cardamom. And pray. I pray for the sales and the children and for God's blessing.

I made over 100 loaves of bread, over 200 cards from my paintings, and I put together over 30 festive baskets to sell . . . It's been a lot, but also lots of fun!

I went to three bazaars and one market, and God has blessed us with making $1210! My SIL Betsy has faithfully come with her wagon to the bazaars and helped set up and tear down. We've had fun chatting with each other, and with the customers... it's been a good thing.

I've made new friends and rekindled acquaintances with other friends, including a penpal from my childhood. (Do people still do penpals? I also have been reacquainted with another penpal who lives here too!)

Sometimes sales were easy, sometimes I made deals or trades, and sometimes God has other plans.

Like the day when sales weren't going that great in the drafty hall next to the bathroom, where we were set up in the back 40. We got a sense that customers were winding down their shopping when they finally hit our wing of the hall. We heard more than one exhausted person actually groan when they saw us, tables laden with more wares to peruse with disdain.

So I "got on the horn," like my dad used to say. The Olson sales lady in me sallied forth! I messaged some friends, who I knew had relatives in the area . . . And they responded positively! I can only say it was a God thing because here's the deal . . . the people I delivered nisu bread and cards and baskets to were so appreciative! It blessed me so much! I felt happy.

Some people were alone. Like the gentleman who used to live on my MIL's road. He now lives in an apartment complex. The sweet old ladies in the lobby told me where to find his room "with the decoration on the door." I asked him if he likes living there and he said, "oh yes, it's warm and quiet." He said his wife had passed years ago, and also his two children, one of whom I knew. I felt a sense of sadness, but he seemed content. He had warmth in his voice when he said he hears from his grandchildren.

Another old guy received me cordially. He didn't know me from Eve, but he invited me in and asked if I wanted coffee. We chatted a bit, his wife slept peacefully in the chair around the corner. He carefully inquired about his friends who gave the gift. We said our "Merry Christmases" and I went on my way.

One gal had been sick on the couch all day; I knocked on the door and heard a dog barking, so I just left the items in a bag on the porch as instructed . . . As I was leaving, the lady came to the door, and we chatted for just a little bit. I learned she has friends but only one daughter in the area. She was so amazed at the gifts from her friend. She lives just a block away from me.

And there were more deliveries, more conversations, more connections.

And I think this was God's plan all along. It kind of brings me to tears. He loves us all so much!—my SIL who is really missing her mom, the old guys and gals in their waning years, young families, single women—and me. God loves us! He blesses us!

I really enjoy connecting with people, hearing their stories, finding commonalities. It binds people together and helps us feel less alone—like there are people who care. We do belong. Our life does matter.

So that's my story—with all its nuances of human expression. We were never meant to do life alone.

So in this season, do the uncomfortable. Follow the urges. Reach out. Someone is waiting to hear from you—and in the process, you will find a blessing.

Arriving in Michigan

Well, here I am, in Chassell, Michigan! Today was just a jaunt from Moose Lake, Minnesota to Chassell. But somehow it took me all day! Now I'm looking forward to spending time here with family and friends.

My day began by hearing loons on the lake! Wow! The water called so I went wading for a while, and then had a yummy breakfast, and a look about in a gift shop. I found one of my favorite old books, Blueberries for Sal! I drove over hills and dales for a while, and met my aunt Chris in Ironwood.

We went to a bakery/pasty shop where grandma would go sometime. She would walk into town and get some goodies or meet a friend and then walk back home. It's nice to know things about our rellies, points of connection.

Then I stopped at my Mattila grandparents old place in Ironwood, and was sorely disappointed by the dilapidated shape of the property. It was so well-kept and beautiful back in the day. So many fun memories. Well, So it goes.

I went on to Wakefield, where I was born, but I couldn't find the hospital. I know I was born there though because I recently saw the receipt for my birth— I think it was $137. I drove around beautiful Sunday Lake and headed toward Berglund, where my parents lived for a time in the '60s. I was the only one not born in Washington of mom and dad's 13 kids. Does that sound confusing?

I smelled pasty cooking so I stopped at Krupps by Twin Lakes for pasties and met a family from Minnesota who are visiting in Michigan. Come to find out they were of the Apostolic Lutheran background also, but we couldn't discover how we were connected. However, he did look like my uncle Bob!

Anywho, that was my day and here I am for a while, looking forward to more good times. Thank you, God, for safe travels.

Walking by the Sea

Ooooh! I was so excited when I read this . . . "Jesus was walking by the Sea of Galilee. . ."

We don't really know if Jesus went there specifically to call Peter and Andrew or maybe he just wanted to walk by the sea. I can relate! I love the ocean; it is so invigorating. Cards and plaques at the beach say, "I go to the sea so I can breathe." Amen?

We were talking about this in prayer group, how we all love to breathe in the ocean air and walk in the sand and the surf. It is exhilarating, refreshing, calming, and lifts our spirits. Upon further discussion, we found there are many physical health benefits—not just mental ones.

Walking barefoot in the sand, or on any natural surface restores electrolytes in our bodies and resets our systems. Breathing in the air, even has a positive effect on our adrenals and our nasal passages. Pretty cool, huh? We knew we loved it, but we didn't know exactly why. But, I thought it was really cool, that Jesus "was walking by the Sea of Galilee" – I love that. I picture him walking by the sea, enjoying it the same as we do. Breathing in the air, enjoying the rolling waves and swooping birds. Watching the changing clouds.

So, next time we go to the ocean I'm going to imagine Jesus there with me, just "walking by the Sea of Galilee," his hair blowing in the breeze, his robe swishing in the sand, his feet making tracks with mine, and his face smiling down at me.

Alignment in the Dishpan

Have you noticed there is something about washing dishes that helps a person gain perspective and alignment?

When my hands are in the dishpan, eyes gazing out the window, thoughts soaring, it seems like I become inspired to "carry on." Actually, it's not really just "carry on," since that kind of sounds like a plodding mule, but it's more like "Go forth!" The Jewish term for that is "Lech L' cha."

Just like Abraham and Sarah went forth into their God-inspired destiny, we too, go forth into ours; whether that means finishing a sinkful of dishes, reading to our children or grands, feeding the homeless, making a joyful noise to the LORD (!), or running for public office. We are encouraged to "Go Forth", "Lech L' cha!"

My prayer for us today is that we all can go forth into our destinies with JOY in our hearts, trusting our mighty El Shaddai. The Almighty One.

And if that means soap bubbles on my fingers, I will be thankful.

Grandma will Travel!

I love spending time with my children and grandchildren. It is hard when they move away; I miss them so much! I work hard so we can get together. Awhile back, one of my daughters and her family moved to New Hampshire, and then to Texas. It has been fun keeping in touch and visiting them.

Their home in New Hampshire was down a country lane lined by rocks, as are many pastures in New England. It's so quaint and beautiful. Their place was perfect for letting kids roam. They had a small pool on the upstairs deck. Once the kids were in the pool, the water was near the top. They were totally impressed when I got in, and the pool flooded over. "Wow," they exclaimed to their mom, "It was so cool! Grandma got in and the water went over the edge!" I guess I'm pretty impressive!

The oldest grandson loved swinging on the swing, hung in the tree near the house. If we ever wondered where he was, we would usually find him on the swing—which is really cool, because swinging is one of the activities that help calm us down and center our brain. He is a very smart boy, who loves to know what's going on. His dad is really good at explaining things to him, and that's amazing. In Texas, they play games in the yard and go to a club for dads and boys. I applaud my sons-in-law. They are good Christian men who care for their families well. This boy pretends to be all tough, but is a softy at heart. He says he doesn't like hugs, but grudgingly asked for a hug when they dropped me off at the airport. He's a sweety! God bless my grandchildren.

When we were in New Hampshire, we went to a butterfly sanctuary, with my sister also. That was a super fun day! The children loved the bugs and butterflies. A butterfly even landed on my oldest grandson's face! He didn't even squawk. His younger brother was in the dirt playing with bugs. He loves bugs! One time he was holding a cricket (a little too tightly I think). When the bug quit moving, he said it had fallen asleep. This little guy is a lover. He will give hugs when necessary. He has the cutest little grin and called his tennis shoes "fast boots." How do kids come up with this stuff? They are amazing!

We went to the beach one day and laughed in the waves. It was so magical! We gathered shells and had a great time. Such sweet memories. The night before we left to go home (a daughter had come with me), we had a fire in the woods. As the fire crackled and popped, we talked about Jesus and roasted marshmallows. These are some sweet memories of their home in New Hampshire.

Texas is good too. We went to the Alamo and floated down the river. We swam under a bridge until sissy thought she spotted a snake. We all got out of the water super quick then. Eek! My daughter is tiny and when she drives the big work truck, it looks hysterical. She goes fast and we all bounce all over the place, the roads have moguls. It's crazy. Life in Texas is different! It feels more wild and free.

There are two big dogs in their little neighborhood and the boys LOVE those dogs. They have friends a few houses down; the children have so much fun together. It's super sweet to listen to them chat and watch them play. I give them candy and they share with their friends. They run in for drinks and grab some fruit when they are hungry. These are the lovely "timeless" days of raising kiddos!

This family has two boys and two girls. The boys are boys and the girls are definitely girls! The girls like sparkles and pink and fancy things. They like to paint and draw. They are all sweet and helpful. It's fun to be with them and watch how God is developing their character as they grow. I wish we could all be together all of the time, but I will cherish the moments we can spend together, treasuring them in my heart.

My Mother: Years at the Sink and the Setting Sun

Awhile back, I was watching the sun setting, glinting through the trees. Rays long, day cold. I was thinking about mom and her life. How she used to sit on her green stool by the sink and look out the farmhouse window (usually slightly open, the white curtains would move gently with the breezes). She would look through her tree, down the driveway and on to the road. She would be peeling a mountain of potatoes for her large family or washing dishes, doing the things a mom does. Thinking, pondering, praying, I'm sure.

The house may have been a hubbub behind her -13 kids doing what kids do. Passing through the kitchen, passing through life. And then moving on. Children grow up, parents grow old.

Now the house is cold and dark, abandoned. Parents and children all gone. The farmhouse walls hold frayed secrets and sweet memories. The house and kitchen seemed cozy then but it was probably shabby and worn. The fire sparked in the winter; the canning pots bubbled in the summer. The kitchen was a place of warmth and good smells. And mom, sitting on her stool.

Often, I too, look out the window as I chop veggies and wash dishes; it is a good place to be alone and reflect. My thoughts wander, I think about things—big and small. Praying. Dreaming.

The long rays of the setting sun reminded me of that. All that was, and is, and is to come. (Is. 46:4; Ps. 71:9; Prov. 22:6; Deut. 6:7)

On the Road Again

There is something that makes me feel bouncy in the morning— getting up early and hitting the road to start a new day feels really good!! So this morning when I set my GPS to Sioux Falls and it said 367 miles, I was like "no problem!"

Farms, horses, cattle. Fields and barns. Gently rolling hills. It rolled on and on. Amazing beauty. Beauty and nature heal our souls. . . Did you know that? God is faithful. I've been listening to good podcasts and sermons also. Enjoying the journey. Creating margin and white space in my life and replenishing my reserves. Letting stuff go and becoming more peaceful. Thanking God.

Well, I really didn't set my GPS to Sioux Falls. I set it to Chevy's restaurant in Sioux Falls! Talk about driving hundreds of miles to go to one of my favorite restaurants!

But before that, I stopped at Wall Drug and got my free ice water and was going to get my five-cent cup of coffee, but I didn't stay long enough for that. I just got a maple donut and a few souvenirs and was on my way again.

Then I started seeing signs for Vivian, South Dakota and I remember stopping there years ago. So I made a detour and drove through this dilapidated town with dirt roads and a house for sale. I wondered if it was a "sign?" Should I buy it?!

I saw an old timer walking a dog and asked him where the nearest restrooms were. He pointed me a mile back down the freeway, so I hopped in my car and hot-footed it down there. I squealed in the back door, ahead of a stream of bikers. Whew!

After driving a bit, I was tired, so I pulled into Luverne Minnesota. Every town has a beat and this one did also. It's an interesting mix with an uptown "fancy" restaurant, an outdoor seating pub with live music, a few motels, a couple fast food joints, a walk-up burger shack, some beautiful homes, a tailgate BBQ going on in the motel parking lot, the Howling Dog tavern, a mom pushing 5 kiddos in swings at the park, one home with "pride" curtains, and a bunch of folks hanging out in the gravel lot waiting for the drive-in movie to start, where I found myself after scoping out the town.

I look around and see a few families and teens . . . and a lot of old duffers, and me—one younger duffer. The family parked next to me just had a moment. Someone passed wind. The teen boy is about ready to die of embarrassment. I can't help laughing. Earlier I had rolled up my windows to do the same! Ha!

Well, it's almost my bedtime and the first movie is about to begin. At least no one will mind if I fall asleep and snore! . . . "The boys of summer" is playing in the background, it's feeling really nostalgic.

Self-Care

Self-care is an attitude of mutual respect. It means learning to live our lives responsibly. It means allowing others to live their lives as they choose, as long as they don't interfere with our decisions to live as we choose. Taking care of ourselves is not as selfish as some people assume it is, but neither is it as selfless as we may believe.

Self-care is an attitude toward ourselves and our lives that says, I am responsible for myself.

I am responsible for living or not living my life.

I am responsible for tending to my spiritual, emotional, physical, and financial well-being.

I am responsible for identifying and meeting my needs.

I am responsible for solving my problems or learning to live with those I cannot solve.

I am responsible for my choices.

I am responsible for what I give and receive.

I am also responsible for setting and achieving my goals.

I am responsible for how much I enjoy life, for how much pleasure I find in daily activities.

I am responsible for whom I love and how I choose to express this love.

I am responsible for what I do to others and for what I allow others to do to me.

I am responsible for my wants and desires.

All of me, every aspect of my being, is important. I count for something. I matter.

My feelings can be trusted. My thinking is appropriate. I value my wants and needs.

I do not deserve and will not tolerate abuse or mistreatment.

I have rights, and it is my responsibility to assert these rights.

The decisions I make and the way I conduct myself will reflect my high self-esteem. My decisions will take into account my responsibilities to myself.

Adapted from "Codependent No More" by Melody Beattie

Heavy Branches

Oh my goodness. God is everywhere and sometimes he gives us moments to revel in his presence. I think he wants us to know he is near and involved in our lives.

Awhile back, I was looking out the window as I often do and noticed the bushes—branches heavy with rain, touching the ground. Not too unusual, until I remembered these branches are usually at least two feet off the ground. Then God started speaking. Isn't it awesome how he does that? He speaks to us through nature.

He reminded me that he works all things for good because we love him and he has called us to good purposes. He reminded me that the rain is necessary for the sustenance of the bushes and plants. And he reminded me that sometimes the heavy "rains" we feel in our lives are also good for us; in fact, necessary for our continued growth.

As I continued to meditate on this bush, I noticed that not only were the leaves of the branches touching the ground, some of them were completely laid out on the ground. And isn't it like that for us sometimes too? We are simply laid out by what life brings. Prostrate on the ground . . . as Jesus once was. He, too, felt the heavy rains and burdens of life—much more than we will ever experience.

Let us remember in our times of "heavy rain" that God is doing a good work. We are fed through the rain and eventually it will stop. And just like the bushes, we will bounce back up, our postures turned up toward the LORD in praise. Just as the branches do, when not weighed down by sustaining rain, they seem to reach for the skies and clap their hands in praise, dancing in joy. . .

Oh, praise you! Praise you Jesus! (Is. 55:12; Heb. 12:8; Matt. 26:36-56)

Oh my Lands

Oh my lands. Or as my small grandson says, "oh my yands." – how precious is that? Oh my yands??!!)

One morning I felt like an old well-used toy with too many springs sprung loose and not enough parts in working order. A toy that at one point had MANY pieces that did marvelous intricate things—all at the same time. But not the other day. Every way I turned, there seemed to be a breakdown in communication somewhere or something boing-ing out at a weird angle. You know what I'm talking about? Ever have those days?

Well, then I decided I needed to go back to the source of all life and goodness and the puter-back-together-er. So, I dragged my ragged parts to the throne and got some prayer for specific areas. Thank you, LORD, for providing that interceder for me. Then through the day, I let God's goodness seep in and all the parts seemed to come back together, boing-ing springs and all.

Later, as I sat talking to a special sister on the phone, she reminded me to work in my area of gifting. She reminded me of the time I went to visit her in Alaska and they got a quarter of a moose from road kill. (That is standard procedure in AK.) So, stomach rolling, I put on an apron, plastic gloves, pulled my hair back and reported for duty. She needed help skinning and cutting the moose into usable pieces. After a few minutes watching her expertly cut through sinew and bone, I took the knife, closed my eyes a little and stuck it in the direction of the moose that was laid out on the table in the yard. Oh my lands. I was not made for this.

Seeing my discomfort, she asked me if I wanted to work on something else. Oh yes!!! . . .So, I painted a mountain scene, complete with a valley and stream on two sides of her chicken coop. That's more like it. That's my area of gifting.

Five years later, the moose meat is long gone, but she told me she still has the chicken house with my painting (moved to another location) reminding her of our good times. As I sat talking to her, the sun had just made its way through the fog and was drying the dew from the leaves that danced in the gentle wind. It looked like thousands of sparkling lights on those beautiful fall trees. Isn't God good?

Later I got to walk through more leaves in the beautiful day with my daughter and her kids. Lovely. Then I was served soup, tea, and cupcakes in the back yard made by my son and grandson. No matter they were made of dirt and water. It was scrumptious.

Oh my yands. Life is good.

On Character in Leadership

As you lead others, character is your most important asset. Character defined is being bigger on the inside. How a leader deals with the circumstances of life tells you many things about his character. Crisis does not necessarily make character, but it reveals it. The meaning of life is not in prospering (as the world sees prospering), but in the development of the soul.

Your character determines who you are. Who you are determines what you see. What you see determines what you do. That is why you can never separate a leaders' character from his actions. Talent is a gift, but character is a choice. We create our character every time we make choices. True leadership brings lasting success with others.

If you think you're leading and no one is following, then you're only taking a walk. Followers do not trust leaders whose character they know to be flawed, and they will not continue following them. People who achieve great heights, but lack the bedrock character to sustain them through stress are headed for disaster. They are destined for one or more of the A's: arrogance, feelings of aloneness, destructive adventure-seeking, or adultery. Each is a terrible price to pay for weak character.

To improve character, do the following:

Search for cracks: identify anywhere you might have compromised or let people down

Look for patterns: is there a particular problem that keeps surfacing?

Face the music: face your flaws, apologize, and deal with the consequences of your actions

Rebuild: face the consequences of past actions and build a new future.

Adapted From John C. Maxwell

Traveling and Thankful

Today I'm thankful for bathrooms at nice visitor centers, Christian cafes, rest during the day, safe travels and cool temps. Tonight it's balmy in Rapid City and it feels nice to be out and about after a swim in the motel pool.

I traveled from the rodeo capital of the world—Cody, Wyoming to Tensleep, an interesting farming community surrounded by craggy high red cliffs, then I ended the day in Rapid City. The night feels soft, with a hazy sky, and an orange sun.

As I traveled toward Tensleep, there were all the things— sassy horses, cattle, huge green fields, old wagons, tractors, and farmers—sporting hats, big belt buckles and genuine cowboy/farming boots. Up close in the Tensleep cafe—Our Daily Bread—the farmers were sunbaked, smiling and seemingly comfortable in their own skin, and in their surroundings. The table of bikers seemed jovial also. It's nice to be around happy people!

I drove through the Big Horn Mountains unexpectedly, and encountered more dazzling beauty. My, oh my!! The rock formations were stunning. The colors changed from dark iron red to white to dark gray— and many variations in between. A person could spend hours taking pictures or drawing or just taking in the majesty.

Some of the rocks were roundish and lumpy, looking like sheep on the hillside, which is interesting because there were signs for bighorn sheep, and obviously the mountain range is named for them, so they must be somewhere. But I didn't see any... Maybe they were just sitting around looking like rocks!

There were also stunted-looking evergreen trees, waterfalls and gorgeous purple lupine. I heard trickling brooks and rushing rivers. Brilliant Bighorn Lake sparkled in the sunshine.

Happy trails!

Philosophy for Positive Approach to Challenges

Accept and give grace—God is the author

Stay in the moment—not past, not future—just this moment

Realize we are all works in progress—act like it

Be thankful in all things—it births joy

Encourage—even tiny steps

Keep in mind, I do not know everything—I am far from perfect

God has created us all for good purposes

He has good paths for each of us to walk in

I am not responsible for others—just me

I can do my part to glorify God by being fully alive to Him and his purposes for me.

(2 Cor. 12: 8-9; Heb. 4:16; John 1:14; Acts 4:33)

Think on what is Pure and Lovely . . .(Phil. 4:8)

If you are struggling with negative thoughts, harmful words, or unhealthy actions, please read and apply the following, it will help immensely. Not that I'm so smart, but I have come into good news that I want to share with you.

In counseling class one night, we were talking about the scripture of "think on what is pure, lovely, of a good report, honest, just, pure, praise-worthy, and virtuous." Our professor/pastor/counselor pointed out that he uses that verse as a filter to process EVERYTHING.

Many times, I have thought about that verse in this context, "Ya, nice concept and I'm trying, but there is so much 'yuck' in the world, that I have to think about (and do something about)." Well, that's a pretty negative unproductive thought but I didn't see a way these two ideas could be compatible. Now I do.

When God gives us a command, it's just that, a command (for our good!). Not a suggestion for those who have achieved a higher level of spirituality. So, taking that verse and applying it to every situation will keep us in perfect peace as our minds are fixed on Him. Furthermore, friends, we ARE responsible for our thoughts—negative or positive, helpful or not. And our thoughts impact our words and actions. It's a great responsibility. Furthermore, thoughts affect the chemical balance (or imbalance in our minds and bodies!) And God has provided a way; he knows positive thoughts produce more positive thoughts, thankfulness, and JOY. So, here's what it looks like in action:

Say a person has been abused. So, is it true? Ok, what is lovely about that? Nothing on first look. But then on a second look what is appealing to the heart or mind about it? Well, God has preserved me. He is using me through and because of the abuse to speak to others. He loves me so much, etc. You see? Then work each thought through all of the words in that scripture and see what amazing things God has done and what He will show you!

And here's another huge concept: It's not so much what happened to us that affects us. It's how we VIEW what has happened to us, and what we MAKE of it - the stories we continually tell ourselves about our world and ourselves. Has the abuse made us feel unlovely? Ok, but what does God say? He calls us Beloved. Set your mind there. Beloved. See how this works? The devil meant the abuse for our harm, but God is using it for good. So, go ahead, start processing EVERYTHING that happens and what has happened through that lens in God's word and see if your thoughts, words, and deeds don't change for the better.

Is that awesome or what? God is good. He always provides a way out. And that's what counseling is all about. Whether it's just talking to a friend and figuring out our situation on our own. Or maybe we need to talk to someone who has been trained to help others find the tools we all need to work through the steps of victim, to survivor to thriver. God wants us to walk in the good paths He has created for us to walk in – as impressive joyful THRIVERS, giving Him all the glory and honor and thanks.

God is Working

God works all things for good, for those who love him and are called according to his purposes. I believe that. I also believe he has good plans for our lives, to give us a future and a hope. And that's just what I told the two young men sitting by the side of the road on my evening walk.

Strolling by their partially rolled down windows, I smelled something funny. I took a few steps and then turned back. "Is that pot I smell?" I asked the young men. Of course, they stumbled around and we bantered back and forth for a while. I could feel my blood pressure rising, as I am so angry about the destructive power of drugs and alcohol to so many lives. I said a quick prayer. God answered. I calmed down and prayerfully said what God wanted me to say.

We talked about many things. The lies drug users believe. The destruction of drugs. How they cloud the mind, derailing goals and futures. I told them I care. I told them some stories of users I have known. There's usually a talker and a silent one, when I end up talking to people about things like this. Talker said he was of age, as he sat there with a big doobbie and the container of dope that he said he bought legally in Vancouver. They were waiting for a friend who lives down the road. I asked them if they were selling. Talker said no and he never would. Your intentions today, I told him, but people end up, down the road doing things, they never thought they would, to support their habit.

I told them God loves them and asked that they would consider what I said. They said I had given them things to think about. I asked if I could pray over them. They said sure. . .

I'm praying heaven came down for them. I asked God to show his sons truth. To show them their/his purpose for their lives. To show them how He loves them. To show them the lies they believed. . .

Did I walk away wishing I would have said something else/different? Yes. Did I wonder if they heard anything I said? Yes. Did I consider if it will make a difference? Yes. But I did the task, the divine appointment. And I'm leaving the outcome to God.

I hope this blesses you – to reach out –wherever you are. To be the hands and feet. God has you right where you are supposed to be. Same as me. He designated my borders long before I was born, for such a time as this – same as you. Keep picking up the gauntlet friends. We fight against principalities and powers of evil. God is NOT dead. He is on the throne. Victorious. He will only allow what he will allow, and then that's it.

Praising Him for allowing us to be part of the divine plan. Praising him for his faithfulness. Blessings! (Rom. 8:28; Eph. 2:10; 1 Cor. 2:10; John 14:26; Jer. 29:11; Rom. 3:23; Heb. 6:1;)

Yellowstone

Thursday in July, I drove through part of Yellowstone Park . . . I'm still in awe!! To think that God created all of this for his pleasure, our enjoyment and as natural resources. It's beauty and expanse are Breathtaking!

It's surreal!! Such amazing beauty. 2.2 million acres! The Highest point is around 11000 feet. It was scary on the edges driving, but there were endless glorious views!! God is amazing! He created all of this!! So humbling.

There was a huge fire there back in 1988. The forests and meadows are regrowing. I saw frolicking elk, a chewing bear, many resting or strolling bison, lots of ducks, and birds. People were courteous. It was a very nice drive. The falls were breathtaking! There were lots of stinky sulfur geysers. Some snow is still by the highway high in the peaks which made sweet little waterfalls, trickling down the mountains. The gorgeous Yellowstone Lake reminded me of Lake Superior. Brilliant wildflowers, verdant meadows, puffy clouds and heavenly skies.

Such majesty!

Yellowstone Park has 10,000 Hot Springs and more than 300 geysers, seven mountain ranges and high plateaus. It also is the habitat of the largest concentration of animals in the lower 48 states with more than 20,000 elk, several thousand bison, hundreds of bears, bighorn, sheep, wolves, moose and deer, and 29 species of mosquitoes!!

Go visit if you can! I didn't see or feel any mosquitoes.

Psalm Ninety-one

How can we experience God's protection, security, and serenity? By dwelling in the shelter of the Most High and resting in the shadow of the Almighty. Ahhhh. Now that's a spa moment! Psalm 91 says when we DWELL in Him, DECLARE our INTENT to trust Him, take REFUGE in His shelter, LOVE Him and

CALL on Him, we WILL experience His protection, even in times of trouble. Praise you Jesus!

So, I went ahead and personalized the last part of the Psalm. I invite you to do the same (experience your Jesus, your resting place, your place of refreshing) :) Blessings to you as you revel in his glory!

"Because Vivian loves me, says the LORD,

I will rescue her;

I will protect her, for she acknowledges my name.

Vivian will call upon me, and I will answer her.

I will be with her in trouble,

I will deliver her and honor her.

With long life will I satisfy Vivian

And show her my salvation."

You are faithful LORD! Praise your name forever. Your faithfulness is my shield and rampart (my defense and walled-in fortification). Bless you name forever.

Ok with Average

I heard some amazing wonderful truths in church that are helping me peel back another layer of the onion. The message I keep hearing lately has to do with letting go, of being ok with something less than stellar.

I have known for years that I am an over-achiever – more, better, best – that's me. Afraid of being mediocre – just a face in the crowd. Every perceived "failure" caused another mark against me. I worked hard, but never hard enough. I labored under the allusion that somehow I had to be something amazing and someone super special. The most excellent grades, the most eye-popping presentations, baker of melt-in-your-mouth dinner rolls, producer of good kids, a successful marriage, excellent relationships, a clean house (all the time), the best encourager, the hardest worker, and a saintly smile at all times, etc etc. . . (I'm exhausted just reading the list!) None of these things is bad; they are worth pursuing. And I told myself, "I'm just being me" as I labored on and on.

The good news for me is this . . . I'm just average and it's ok . . . Whew! Today's society (even our Christian society) has taught us that we have to be successful in every arena. We are continually pumping each other up – in our "super specialness." And I do agree with that, to a degree. Each person is special and amazing and created in the image of God. But the word I heard was refreshing—most of us are not superstars. We are just average people doing an average job. How incredible to let it all go. . .

And in the wake of all the pumped-up, puffed-up superhero status, is an incredible peace. But the amazing news is this— God wants to be WITH us. He is the one who makes anything we do super or special. He is the one who shines. He is the One with whom we are in relationship as we "pray without ceasing." He is Emmanuel—God WITH us.

He came as a baby, to meet us in our humanity. He came and became sin, so our sin and shame can be removed. He left heaven so that we could enter the pearly gates. That's our God. The One who desires to be with us. Emanuel.

I am just average and it's ok. That's the word I heard. Not a superstar, super special, over-achieving wonder woman who rocks every corner of her world. Just an average person (who makes mistakes sometimes ((sometimes more than sometimes)). And it's ok. What a relief!

Bubbles and Beauties

Three of my little granddaughters came over one afternoon for a spa day with grandma. I had planned, shopped and prepped. Everything was ready. A gift for each, which we would use during our time together.

We turned on the soft music and they took turns soaking their tiny toes in bubbles. Then grandma gave them a foot massage and new socks. Next, I lotioned up their hands and gently rubbed their little fingers. We combed hair and put in pretty hair bobbles. They put on some of my lovely scarves.

Then we created some magic and did some arts and crafts— glueing, cutting, sparkles.

Next it was time for special snacks. We used the tea set that I had packed into a pretty hat box for one of the girls' presents. It was all so sweet and lovely. The were perfect dainty ladies as they sipped their tea and ate their cakes and fruit. It was fun to see them sipping and appreciating the fine things in life. We listened to music and giggled about funny things.

After awhile, we packed that away. It was time to read a story. Then we started watching a favorite movie, all snuggled together under a blankie on the couch.

My heart was full. Time with these little princesses is priceless. They are the true treasures of life!

A few months later, they returned the favor and asked me to tea! They had helped their mommy get the pretty dishes out, cut the fruit and make the sandwiches. The tea was sweet and delicious. I was honored by their special gift.

Spa days, tea parties, even days just folding clothes together. I'm so thankful for the time we get to spend with each other. It's a beautiful life! Thank you, Lord!

Pendleton to Idaho Falls

Today was beautiful all around, but I had three major highlights of my day as I traveled from Pendleton to Idaho Falls! I found a little fruit stand out in the middle of the corn fields. A gal had prepped luscious fruit and had it on ice, and when you drove up, she made a fruit salad to your specifications... It was refreshing and so delicious!

Then I drove further into town, (I got on the back roads) and I found Me Me's Boutique! Me Me is a miracle cancer survivor, a descendent of the Arapaho Indians, and has more wrinkles than anyone I have ever seen—She glows beautifully! We agreed that God is good, and she blessed me on my trip, and I was on my way.

At the Summit of the Blue Mountains the elevation was 4100 feet. Blue skies, puffy, clouds, evergreens. La Grande is beautiful also. Hills all around the gorgeous valley farming communities.

I saw so many farms, and mountains in the distance. I pulled off the freeway and drove down a back road. People actually wave at you; four wheelers were going down the road working on the farms. There was a stockyard, cow hides on a fence, irrigation ditches, combines on the road, stacks of hay—its growing season in America. This was just over the Oregon/Idaho border. There are endless fields, cows and horses and huge fields of dusty sandy soil.

And one big airplane parked in Mountain Home, Idaho. The hills of Idaho hold historic gold mines. It looks like they get mountains of snow up in this area, but summertime there are a lotta cattle grazing in peaceful meadows. Blue lakes with floating ducks. Then there were lava fields called "craters of the Moon."

I drove through more stunning country and saw many farms and other cool things. Then, at the end of the day I stopped in Idaho Falls. This was my third high point of the day, along with the fruit stand and Me Me. The town had dammed up the Snake

River to create power, and they created these gushing falls that cascade, seemingly for half a mile... It's so gorgeous! There's also a beautiful walkway for people to enjoy it all. Folks were out and about, walking, skating, eating and enjoying the balmy evening.

Then I had some yummy rosemary, raspberry vinaigrette chicken salad and chocolate cake! I like to look online and see where the best places are to eat and also to check out the highlights of area—I'm so glad I stopped in Idaho Falls.

Good night. Sweet dreams. Say your prayers. God is faithful and true—always and forever.

Tidings of Comfort and Joy

Sometimes we confuse happiness and joy. Happiness depends on happenings - unwrapping the gifts, laughing over a good story, an unexpected bonus. Joy depends on Christ. "Running deeper and stronger, joy is the quiet, confident assurance of God's love and work in our lives" so says my Bible commentary.

Philippians is Paul's letter of joy, joy even in suffering. That's what we need the "comfort" for - the tribulations of this life. One day all will be renewed and well. But for now, even in our trials, we have joy because Jesus lives in our hearts. We spend our days with our best friend. Don't you love that! Hallelujah!

Even when the gifts do not meet our expectations, even when the joke is on us, even when we are struggling financially. Because of the gift of the Christmas season, we are joyful.

For me, this joy is the confident assurance of God's faithfulness. But it is encapsulated in a bubble deep inside - my joy bubble. One day, that joy bubble is going to grow so big, so warm, so full of Jesus it will burst open, just like a gigantic soap bubble. And all the beautiful colors are going to explode in magnificent splendor. And then heaven will begin for me. That's what my joy bubble looks like.

I hope you have a joy bubble. What does it look like? What does it feel like?

Tidings, of comfort . . . and joy!

Be of Good Cheer

"These things I have spoken unto you, that in me ye might have peace. In the world ye shall have tribulation: but be of good cheer; I have overcome the world." John 16:33. Amen?

Wow! What comfort God gives us through His word. What peace He gives us with His presence—the Holy Spirit—the comforter who is guiding us in all truth. We have tribulation! Yes, how well I know it. Without digging too deeply, many situations come to mind where there is major tribulation—in my family, in the lives of my extended family, among my close friends. Tribulation abounds! But, Jesus has spoken peace into our hearts and minds! His name is faithful and true. He is WITH us—Emmanuel!

Look UP, dear friends, in the midst of your tribulation. Your God, the faithful ONE is fighting for you. He is speaking peace into your troubled hearts and lives. Hallelujah! As the sun shines into the windows of my home, it reminds me of God's faithful love and presence.

I pray we can ask God for a fresh revelation of His warm love, that we can let the rays of His presence fill us with peace—even in the midst of our tribulation. Be of good cheer. He has assured us that this ends well. Be blessed. He is faithful who promised.

Emotional Competence begins in the Cradle

"The impact of parenting on emotional competence starts in the cradle."

"A child's readiness for school depends on the most basic of all knowledge, *how* to learn. [The report lists the] seven key ingredients of this crucial capacity – all related to emotional intelligence..."

Confidence - "A sense of control and mastery of one's body, behavior, and world; the child's sense that he is more likely than not to succeed at what he undertakes, and that adults will be helpful."

Curiosity - "The sense that finding out about things is positive and leads to pleasure."

Intentionality - "The wish and capacity to have an impact, and to act upon that with persistence. This is related to a sense of competence, of being effective."

Self-Control - "The ability to modulate and control one's own actions in age-appropriate ways; a sense of inner control."

Relatedness - "The ability to engage with others based on the sense of being understood by and understanding others."

Capacity to Communicate - "The wish and ability to verbally exchange ideas, feelings, and concepts with others. This is related to a sense of trust of others and of pleasure in engaging with others, including adults."

Cooperativeness - "The ability to balance one's own needs with those of others in group activity."

"All the small exchanges between parent and child have an emotional subtext, and in the repetition of these messages over the years, children form the core of their emotional outlook and capabilities."

"The risks are greatest for those children whose parents are grossly inept – immature, abusing drugs, depressed or chronically angry, or simply aimless and living chaotic lives. Such parents are far less likely to give adequate care, let alone attune to their toddlers' emotional needs."

Abuse – the extinction of empathy - "...meanness in place of empathy is typical of...children...who are already, at their tender age, scarred by severe physical and emotional abuse at home." Notes from Daniel Goleman's "Emotional Intelligence"

**"I don't sing because I'm happy.
I'm happy because I sing."**
This was quoted in my Assertiveness class at Clark College. Or, like the Bible indicates, thankfulness fosters joyfulness. So, how does one move from despondency to joyfulness?

We were talking about the power of positive thinking in class. One guy said, "Fake it, til you make it." He said it takes him a couple hours of gritting his teeth and pretending to be feeling great until he actually feels good. Another guy (who had something to say about almost everything!) said he listens to positive thinking CD's. Others offered similar suggestions. What has been your experience?

Today, I'm going to dwell on thankfulness. I'm thankful for . . . rain falling on the top of my house, instead of on top of my head. . . my health, even though my allergies are trying to take me down . . . friends coming tonight to celebrate a sister's accomplishment. . . . opportunities . . . the many blessings of family . . . the mental capacity to do things differently . . . . interesting classes I'm taking at Clark . . . the transforming power of prayer . . . God's power that moves my thinking to be in line with God's thinking . . . a brain that's even able to meditate on such things. . . eyes to see the beauty of God's creation . . .

So, what's at the top of your thankfulness list today? Or, what has moved you from lying on the couch with a pillow over your head to singing your heart out?

Goldendale

It might've been my detour to get this amazzzing purple passion Lotus energy drink that got me in trouble in the first place, but I think it was worth it . . .

The scenery around Goldendale is breathtaking! (Even though it's just a little bit longer to reach my destination, it's a fun place to travel through.) God sure did an incredible job creating this old world. "Oh, beautiful for spacious skies, for amber waves of grain" and all that!!

Well, it really wasn't "trouble" I got into, but more a sense of being all alone in the world, in the middle of the desert, high on a cow path, with limited gas in my tank—just a minor blip!

You see, I was taking the country road from Pasco to Goldendale to hit this remarkable coffee/energy drink shop, then I continued on down to Hood River, but I chose route 142 on my GPS, which was basically a cow trail through the highest point on the mountain pass, I'm convinced. It was kind of scary, being that high up in the world, with only a teeny rail between me and a deep ravine!

So I'm tooling along, watching the rail and the range of my gas tank dwindle on my dashboard (I started feeling a little cross-eyed with the endeavor!) It looked like I had enough fuel to make it to the main road but then I tried to "add a stop" on the GPS for gas, and it said "no search available." Well, whatever. I said a prayer and continued along the trail (sure enough I found a cow or two!)

I was getting a little nervous, but then the cow path widened, and I heard the peaceful sound of water and found the Klickitat River! Even though it was an odd shade of greenish-brown, water is still water and it had its beauty. I followed it awhile, eye still on my gas gauge.

The desert flowers along the road were lovely. The sky a beautiful summer sapphire. A few eagles or eagle-ish birds floated in the air. It was all quite enchanting. Except for that gas gauge. But I knew it was probably going to be ok, right???

Then lo and behold, I rounded the corner and there were signs of life. Human life. And a sign stating "Klikitat." Will wonders never cease? There in the desert, seemingly doing nothing but sitting there looking so attractive (and kinda ugly too) was this little town.

I quickly tried to look for a gas station again, on my GPS and found nothing. So I continued on... I like to check things out and see how people live. And, I'm driving along, no gas station in sight. But suddenly out of the corner of my eye I saw a pump. A pump. One. I whipped around and thankfully started pumping my gas. Even at $4.99 a gallon, I was grateful.

I popped back into my steady steed and continued my journey, purple passion drink long gone. Head still gazing side to side. Just enjoying the gorgeousness. Blasting City Alight, shouting how the enemy can't take what we have or change who we are because we belong to God!!! Glory!

Feeling so loved and thankful for God's faithfulness and that lone gas pump in the desert.

I know He doesn't have to do all this for us, for me—but I think He likes to. I think it gives Abba pleasure when we trust Him to thrill us in ways big and small.

It's true what the Bible says, He takes us into the desert so he can "speak "tenderly to us.

Grandma Glory

The small man toddles across the yard, arms and hands swinging; he knows right where he's going—to the mud and water filled pans sitting on the play kitchen (just like any small man would). Grandma runs to the rescue and quickly dumps out the water, and scurries to the shed to fill up his bucket with white play sand. He promptly scoops it out and dumps it on the ground—making a beautiful mountain. He's completely fascinated by the white grains running out of his cup onto the ground. Mama says, "Hunny, don't dump it on the ground, dump it in a pot," (just like any mother would).

Grandma sits on the stoop and watches the little dumpling, completely spellbound by the discovery process going on in his little head. (Spellbound, just like any grandma would be). Little boy is completely oblivious to anyone or anything besides his sand; he is miles away in Erickson's autonomy vs. shame/doubt stage or Piaget's sensorimotor stage. However, grandma knows whatever the psychologists want to call it, its pure discovery. He is learning how his world works and how he fits into that world. This is the groundwork for a solid foundation to the man he will be one day.

The cat jumps up on him. He looks a little nervous and exclaims, "Kitty!" Mama thinks he may be remembering the tigers from the zoo. Mama says good-bye, baby flaps at her as she leaves; he's still engrossed in the sand. After a while grandma heads into the house and the little one follows. Once inside, grandma turns away for a moment, then little Mr. hooks one sweet little inquisitive finger into just the right size hole in the crocheted tablecloth and pulls it all so nicely onto the floor—a perfectly executed landslide. A teacup and saucer, papers, and other junk go piling to the floor! "Oh baby!" exclaims Grandma as she turns away to get something to clean off the now exposed dirty glass tablecloth. "Maamaw," he says with a certain tone in his voice.

Maamaw turns around and the little imp hands her a $600 pair of glasses that had been nicely sitting out of reach up on the table. Heaven sakes! What next? That mess is cleaned up and the evening passes in a swirl of sticky sippy cups, uneaten supper, bath time, poopy diapers, and splattered yogurt.

Later, snuggling before bed with the little chap and his fuzzy, doggy, and stack of favorite books, Maamaw realizes she ain't as young as she usta be. However, she is a lot wiser and has more love in her heart and she thinks that might be a better trade, after all.

About 3 in the morning, all that love and wisdom come to the rescue when the little one cries in the night. This isn't an interruption of sleep, but a moment to spend more time snuggling with the short man who has wedged himself completely into a large corner of her thankful heart.

Much of Life is a Paradox

Much of life is a paradox. The tension between the known and the unknown. Understanding the sovereignty of God and our ability to choose. We see in part, but one day face to face.

Today, the things that are revealed belong to us; the rest belong to God.

Even in relationship, we see only what we see and know.

There's a concept called Johari's Window which explains that we all have an area even in our own identity, that we do not know—it's what others know about us, but we do not know ourselves—our blind spots. Scary stuff—asking or seeking to know what others know about us that we do not. It makes us feel vulnerable and exposed.

However, truthfully, the exposed parts are already known to others, just not to us. See how it? Even in this, the tension between the known and the unknown. The mystery and the reality. It's what came to mind this morning as I was thinking about our sovereign God (He is in control), who allows us choice.

We have choice in many areas of our lives, yet He is sovereign. It's a holy mystery.

Granddaughters

Grandchildren really are the icing on the cake, and granddaughters make it so super sweet! I have quite a few now and they all are so special!

One of them is growing up so fast. She's so accomplished and smart. Still years from being a teenager, she knows how to do so much. Her mother has taught her and her siblings well. She makes yummy cakes, washes dishes, cleans the bathroom and feeds the chickens. She's competitive and athletic—a whiz on her bike. She works hard to keep up with her brother and is so determined not to be left in the dust. I can relate!

She loves drawing and painting, making forts and playing in the woods. One day I arrived to their place, and the children were busy making their fort homey with moss. Other times, they had made a bridge over their little creek and were playing dress-up games. When they come to my house, they love wearing my scarves and jewels, mixing colored "potions" in my little glass jars and painting faces. They leave behind their precious rocks and pictures and special toys.

This little lady loves to come help me when I make food and deliver it to people. They appreciate her also and give her treasures. Our time together is priceless. We sing songs and tell stories. When she comes with me, she is my little secretary who takes care of my money, receipts, bags and tags. Once, we got into the car after getting some items at a fun re-sale shop and I handed her my things to sort and put in the appropriate places. I said, "Thank you! I'm glad I have a helper." She smiled back, "You're welcome" her little hands full of receipts and money. Then she made us both laugh by adding, "I need a helper!"

Another time while riding in the car. I said, "Let's sing. What's your favorite song?" She stated, "Jesus keep me near the cross." I asked, "You know that song?" She replied, "Yes, Daddy sings with us in the car and we learned it together." So, I googled it and we sang. She knew it by heart. It made my heart so happy! —and so thankful her Daddy sings with them. A month or so later, all of the children were with me and we went to a favorite aunt's house and sang it with her. They are such a blessing! Father, please keep them in your tender care.

Tennessee Travel

I will miss these peaceful country roads, and the mellows Tennessee vibe, the sleek cattle grazing in sweeping pastures, the barns, the flowers, gnarled trees, the gentle mountains and lazy rivers. I will miss sister Jo and her sweet family. The fun, snacks, games, swimming, laughter, stories and tears.

There's a dark spot on a country lane close to their home that we drive around. That's where her son Jonny found his portal to heaven. Tears and laughter, comings and goings, the rhythm of life continues until that glad day that's coming soon... In the meantime we will continue to enjoy all that God has given us. This is the day that the Lord has made. I will rejoice and be glad in it.

A shore drive away is Townsend, Tennessee. They are fighting hard to maintain their peaceful smallish town. Today I visited the Great Smoky Mountain Heritage Museum in Townsend. The buildings are from original farmsteads. People sure had to work hard! Everybody had a garden so they could eat. Women tended the gardens, men worked in the fields. They also cultivated roses and other flowers and herbs for beauty and medicine.

Usually, homes consisted of one room with a bed, fireplace, a work table and maybe a cabinet or two, a few chairs, and sometimes a loom for making carpets and a trunk for clothes. Some pioneer homes had an inside staircase, or sometimes they just had a ladder to reach additional sleeping quarters upstairs. It's all so interesting— I wonder how I would have done living back in the day??

Later my sister and her husband and I had a fun float down the Little River. It was so peaceful to float and then to rest in the grass and look at the beautiful blue sky and the brilliant fluffy clouds. It was a nice end to the day, visiting with some peeps on cozy chairs overlooking the river. God bless us all in the beautiful world He created.

His Banner Over me is Love

"Praise the Lamb for sinners slain! Give Him glory all ye people, for His blood can wash away each stain." That's the song that God put in my heart recently.

What is your song? Your personal love sonnet from Your redeemer? You have one, you know. He says He surrounds us with songs of deliverance. Have you ever wondered about those songs?

With all of its ups and downs, life happens, right? Sometimes it's a giddy twirl on top of a mountain and other times it's a slow slide DOWN the mountain, over boulders and scratchy bushes. Sometimes we feel like we can fly on the wings of the morning and other times we wonder if morning will ever come. But, through it all, our God surrounds us with songs of deliverance. How amazing is that? I've been contemplating that lately – those songs of deliverance.

Even though, sometimes I feel like I've landed on a jagged boulder with a blackberry vine scratching my derriere, God has put a song in my heart! The Bible says His banner over us is love, He sings over us, and surrounds us with songs of deliverance. What a God! The word also tells us that He lives in the praises of His people—He LIVES in the praises of His people. He wants us to sing our songs of deliverance! Praise you, Jesus!

Oh, somehow, I'll have to get off my prickly perch, but the Bible reminds me that we are more than conquerors through Christ. Not just conquerors, but MORE than conquerors. Well, how can we be more than what we are? Through Christ. All things are possible with Him; no matter what tangle or mess we are in. He gives us our songs of deliverance—His letter of love and redemption, the songs of David, the promises of His word. Hallelujah!

I don't know what your particular challenges in life are, but something I struggle with is being appropriate. I am very spontaneous and, well, sometimes I just say something or do something that might be a little off. So then the devil bludgeons me with how inappropriate I am. Well, maybe, sometimes. But now I've learned to run to Abba when I feel wounded. I confess my weights and sins to Him, and the One whose name is Faithful and True heals me. And gives me a song of deliverance.

Just to encourage you wherever you are—mountaintop or boulder-straddled, your Creator's banner of love is over you and He surrounds you with songs of deliverance! So, until the day when He gives us a new song to sing, rest in His love, His promises, and His songs of deliverance. Praise the Lamb for sinners slain!

Sisu

I am Finnish. My great grandparents came from Finland to escape extreme poverty and to find a better life. Even living in America was hard for Finns, back in the day. They labored from sunup to sundown just to make a meager living. They had a lot of sisu and it's in my DNA.

Sisu is a Finnish term loosely translated into English as strength of will, determination, perseverance, and acting rationally in the face of adversity.

In fact, one of my great-grandmas sailed to New York ahead of her husband; she worked hard. Little by little, she saved enough money to send back to Finland for her beloved to join her. Another great-grandma settled in Otter Lake, Michigan. Every day, she looked out over the water and cried. It reminded her so much of the homeland and family she had left behind. As a young woman, she left knowing she would never see them again. Another grandpa delivered mail on foot. An easy job in the summer, but wading through deep snowbanks in the winter was another matter. Sometimes, he was so exhausted, he came home on his hands and knees. And every day, these ancestors of mine, got up and did it again. That's sisu.

The word sisu is widely considered to lack a proper translation into any language. Sisu has been described as being integral to understanding Finnish culture. The literal meaning is equivalent in English to "having guts," and the word derives from sisus, which means something inner or interior.

However, sisu is defined by a long-term element in it; it is not momentary courage, but the ability to sustain an action against the odds. Deciding on a course of action and then sticking to that decision against repeated failures is sisu.

It is similar to equanimity, except the forbearance of sisu has a grimmer quality of stress management than the latter. The noun sisu is related to the adjective sisukas, one having the quality of sisu.

I am thankful for my ancestors and all that they accomplished and endured. I am a better person because of them and their stories. Most of all, I am thankful for the abiding spirit, which also resided in them. We will meet one day in Glory, and that will be amazing!

Tips for Maintaining a Positive Attitude

Read and Listen to Positive Messages! One of the best ways to maintain a positive attitude is by reading positive books and listening to good music. They will encourage you, inspire you, and teach you.

Wake up Early. Create the habit of waking up early. It gives us a head start on the day. During this time, we can spend time reading or in prayer or meditation, or even take a relaxing bath!

Exercise. It makes a huge difference in our physical health and mental health—it helps put a bounce in our step, and it dispels gloom and depression.

Create goals. Having a plan can help you maintain a positive attitude. By knowing what you want to accomplish you will be able to focus on your important life priorities.

Understand that Things Won't Always Go as Planned. If you plan and expect everything in life will go as you planned, you will be quickly disappointed. One of the keys to maintaining a positive attitude is to understand that things will go wrong. If you expect things to go wrong, you will not be put off course when they do.

Get the proper nutrition and supplements. Eat plenty of fruits, veggies and protein. Avoid empty calories, that just make us feel bad. Drink lots of water and take supplements as needed.

Get Spiritually Connected. This might mean prayer, meditation or reading Scripture. Set aside time each day to get connected spiritually. The benefits will be amazzzing!

Be Thankful. Take some time and be thankful. Be thankful about what you have, who you are, and what your life is like. Think through all of the things for which you can be thankful. Even if we are in a tough time in life, there are many things for which we can give thanks. God lives in the praises of his people! And it changes the chemicals in our brain to be more positive.

Surround Yourself with Positive People. The people around you have a big impact on you. They influence who you are and what you value. They also affect how you think.

Singing Blessings over your Home

I just wanted to share something I heard in church that really sank into my heart. It's so beautiful. I went to a different church during Christmas-time and the preacher was sharing about Mary's prayer. He brought out how she was magnifying the Lord.

He said that the song of the redeemed (her song) is even more beautiful than the song of Adam and Eve when they were first in the Garden. The song of the redeemed. Like Mary. Wow!

Through God's amazing grace I know the songs of the redeemed! Hallelujah!

The pastor said his mother and grandmother used to sing as they worked around their homes, and as the little children played, and did what they needed to do, the mothers' song—the song of the redeemed was a blessing over the children—singing the songs of Zion.

It just warmed my heart. How lovely is that?!

So mothers raising your children, (and all of us) may this encourage you to sing as you go about your daily work. You are blessing your home and your children. I know life isn't always easy, and sometimes we definitely don't feel like singing. But God encourages us to sing. He lives in the praises of his people! And I know from experience, and listening to my mother sing over the dishpan, it is most definitely a peaceful blessing—for everyone.

It changes the atmosphere of the home, and just as important, it changes the atmosphere of our heart and mind. And it's also a beautiful incense to God. I just love that.

May this encourage and bless you all.

"Redeemed—how I love to proclaim it! Redeemed by the blood of the Lamb; Redeemed through His infinite mercy, His child, and forever, I am. Redeemed, redeemed!"

The Old Gray Barns of Cove Creek

"Come set awhile," invited the sweet-looking elderly woman as she patted a chair on her porch.

I had been driving along the old beaten path, camera hungrily recording aged houses and barns, flowers, horses grazing in meadows, and so much more! The quaint beauty of the mountain cove was taking my breath away and stealing my heart. I could hardly contain my excitement, and then I saw the white-haired woman sweeping her tidy porch.

Gingerly I pulled into her grassy driveway. Lovely flowers bobbed in the breeze. The purple and red plants were hiding three or four graying sheds, tucked along a bubbling brook.

This whole valley was almost unbelievable. It was so picturesque! —the scenes of calendars and puzzles, stories, and treasured coloring books.

I introduced myself and so did Ida (names have been changed). She called for her husband Emil to join us on the porch.

Just off Highway 321 in the Appalachian Mountains lies the community of Cove Creek, population 1171, dating back hundreds of years. Dating back to the days when most folks were poor and lived off the land. They helped each other when a neighbor fell on hard times. Community wasn't just a buzzword, but a way of life.

"A way of life that is long gone," says Emil, gazing up the tree-canopied winding mountain road. Emil and Ida have lived in this community for a very long time. They remember days gone by.

"They were good days, but hard days," continued Emil. "We were all poor, but nobody thought about it much, we were in it together." His white beard and the lines along his cheeks spoke to many years well-lived in his mountain home, tending crops. In later years, he worked on the road crew until retirement.

Then they were able to travel to many states, including my own—Washington. Again, they were drawn to the mountains; seeing Mt. St. Helens was a highlight of their trip.

In the cove, the numerous old houses, inspiring barns and sheds dotting the landscape hold secrets and memories. Their mellow boards sag gently in the weather, dignified remains of another time.

Ida, eyes merry and blue, remembers times past—times of planting and harvest. The buildings are now used to store supplies and wood that has been chopped to last through the cold mountain winters, she shares. Many old homes are either still occupied, or remain on the family property, too dear to be demolished.

Emil explains that the mountain folks grew tobacco, potatoes and cabbage back in the day. The sheds would hold the harvest until it was brought to market. He also remembers his grandfather raising sheep further up the valley. Some farmers down the road had cows, but mostly they raised plants and produce. In later years, there were four factories in their area, all long gone now. The old community milkhouse is now an ornamental nursery, providing plants and flowers to tuck into pots and place in the ground next to porches and barns.

The charming brook bubbles on in a timeless rhythm, flowing down from the mountain passes. It flows past the barns that hold memories, and maybe a faint smell of tobacco. It gurgles past homes, abandoned with age, windows looking for the family to return. It continues on down to the large Watauga Lake where young people are creating new traditions of boating, fishing and swimming with their friends and families.

Emil, Ida and I sat a bit longer on the porch, savoring the by-gone memories.

Soon it was time for me to go.

Amidst smiles and goodbyes, I drove away, thinking that the earlier way of life may have been more soul-satisfying than the hustle and bustle that most of us live today.

The past way of life seemed to create strong resilient folks who knew how to live off the land. They knew how to support one another and live harmoniously together. They knew how to preserve their culture. And they knew how to invite a stranger to come, "set awhile" and experience the past for a few poignant moments in the shadow of bygone days and old gray barns.

**Well done, thou good and faithful Anita
Enter into the Joy of the Lord!!**

Tribute to Anita Walikainen,
mother, grandma, friend,
you've lost the ties to earth
as the Lord called you home.
the sun rose between the trees
and you slipped away at dawn.
your soul rose beyond the clouds
your sweet spirit left this earth
you've loved us, oh, so well,
your leaving is deeply felt.
your mom sang to you of faith and home,
your pa taught patience, love and hope.
your Bible was your anchor,
goodness and kindness were your robes.

your children call you blessed,
to your grands you were the best!
presents tucked away in presents
pancakes and root beer floats.
money in stockings
walks in the woods
petting the dogs
saunas and reading books.
we loved to visit you in your place,
your home was blessed and sweet.
the rooms were always ready
the toys set out so neat.
you flew to us for parties, babies, weddings,
and all events great and small.
we ironed the sheets,
the kids wrote notes
we counted the days
and then grandma arrived in the plane!
you never spoke harshly
your essence was sisu and love.
your life was such a blessing
your friendship was a gift from above.
we knew this day would come
but, Nita, it's so hard!
you loved with so much grace
you treated us so well!
to use the prose of a child—
we loved you since we knew you.
there never will be another
quite like you, dear sister, friend, mother.
Vivian Walikainen daughter-in-law

Well, readers, that's it for now. Thanks for "rambling" along with me. It's been fun looking back, looking around and looking forward. But most importantly, let's always remember to look UP—into the face of Jesus, looking full into His wonderful face! —To see HIM, enthroned in the heavens, in all of His glory and grace! . . . Blessings and love until next time, Gramma V